# DEALING WITH HEALING

*Healing Trauma Impacts Your Professional Performance*

OLIVIA SMITH, RN

Write A New Story
Write A New Story, LLC

Tennessee, USA

ISBN: 979-8-9939292-1-7

Printed in the United States of America

# CONTENTS

# Dedication

This book is dedicated to my biological mother for the gift of life and my adoptive parents and brother, who changed my life.

To my legacy, my children, Mary Olivia, and Laura, who model grace and unconditional love beyond my understanding.

To my love, my husband, who keeps me safe by covering me in his perfect love every day.

And to the light, the women of Healing Housing, who are choosing to write their new stories one day at a time. Your courage shines rays of light on the healing path, so others may have the courage to follow in your footsteps.

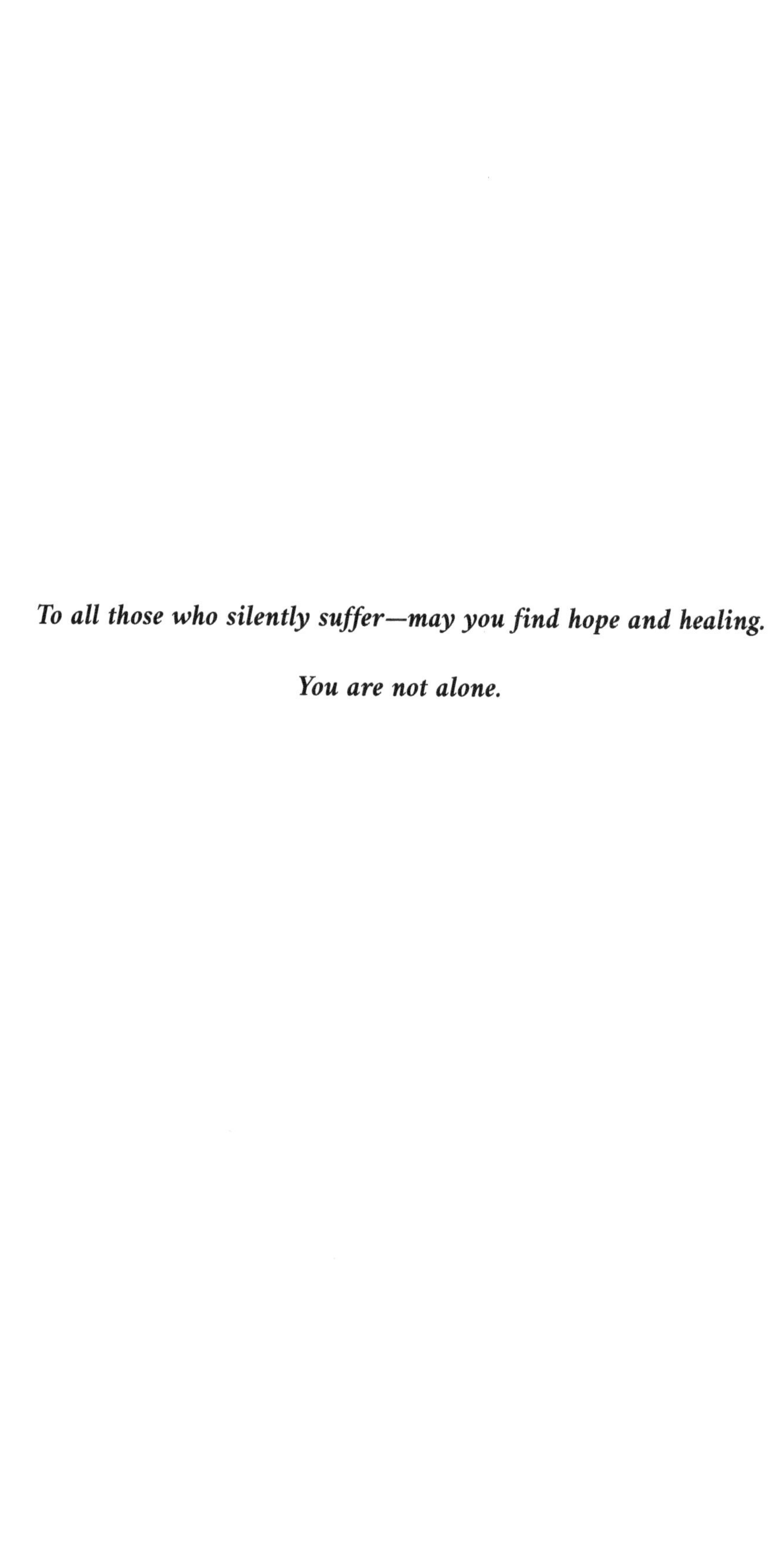

*To all those who silently suffer—may you find hope and healing.*

*You are not alone.*

# Introduction

Trauma is like a shadow, always present, whether you acknowledge it or not. You can push it out of sight and obscure it beneath the weight of success or busyness, but shadows don't disappear because we choose not to look at them. They move with us, influencing our choices, interactions, and even how we see ourselves. They linger in the subtle ways we hesitate to speak up in a meeting, the unexplainable knot of anxiety before a big decision, or the moment we overreact to constructive feedback.

The real question isn't how long you can ignore it but how much it's already costing you. What parts of yourself, your confidence, creativity, or connection with others, are you unknowingly sacrificing by leaving trauma unaddressed? And what happens when you finally turn toward the shadow, not to fight it but to understand it?

This book is an invitation to stop running from the past and start writing a new story. While trauma may shape us, it doesn't have to define us.

Have you ever paused to wonder why certain challenges feel insurmountable or why some professional relationships seem so much harder than others? For many of us, the answer lies obscured in our past. Nearly 70 percent of adults have experienced at least one significant adversity or trauma in their lives, and the impact often lingers long after the event is over. Trauma doesn't vanish when the immediate crisis passes; it takes root, shaping how we navigate relationships, careers, and even our self-perception.

But we're often reluctant to acknowledge it. For high-achieving professionals, it's easier to focus on climbing the ladder, growing a business, or earning accolades. We convince ourselves that trauma is a private matter, neatly tucked away in our personal lives, separate from the boardroom or office. Yet the truth is that unresolved trauma seeps into every corner of our lives. It shows up as chronic stress, impostor syndrome, strained workplace relationships, or even burnout. It whispers doubts, erodes confidence, and if left unchecked, can sabotage our success.

Ignoring trauma is like neglecting a leak in the roof. At first, it seems manageable—a small patch here, a little caulk there. But over time, that leak drips down into the support beams, weakening the entire foundation. By the time the damage becomes visible, it's often far more extensive than we ever imagined. And sometimes, the foundation simply crumbles from the weight it can no longer bear.

The good news is that healing is possible. It doesn't only restore what was broken; it can build something stronger. By addressing our trauma, we can reclaim the parts of ourselves that felt lost or broken, turning pain into resilience and authenticity. In doing so, we not only heal, grow, thrive, and unlock our full potential but also become more resilient.

This book isn't about "getting over it." It's about facing it. It's about finding the courage to look at what's been hidden and learning to write a new story, one where you're in control of the narrative. Healing is a deeply personal process, and there's no one-size-fits-all solution. What works for one person may not work for another. That's why this book offers insights and stories from a diverse selection of real people who've turned their pain into power, showing you that healing is not only possible but also a transformative process worth embarking on.

The stories that follow include candid accounts of trauma, abuse, and recovery. Some descriptions may be triggering. Please read gently and seek professional support if needed.

According to research published in the *Journal of Business Research,* adversity and resilience don't follow a straight line. Researchers have found that those who have faced moderate levels of adversity often demonstrate greater creativity, resourcefulness, and long-term professional success. In other words, the experiences that feel most painful can also spark the qualities that drive achievement—once they are acknowledged and healed.

Similarly, research highlighted in *Creative Education* shows that many top-performing leaders have transformed personal trauma into extraordinary influence. Their stories remind us that healing is not only an inward journey; it can also fuel leadership, strengthen relationships, and create a legacy far beyond our dreams.

As a former nurse, entrepreneur, and leadership consultant, I've spent my life in spaces where trauma reveals itself in unexpected ways. In the trauma unit, I saw families grappling with unimaginable loss. In business, I worked with leaders who, despite outward success, carried the invisible weight of their past into every decision they made. Through my work with Healing Housing, a transitional living program for women in recovery, I witnessed the extraordinary transformations that occur when people confront their trauma with honesty and support.

Through these varied life experiences, one truth has become clear: Trauma is not a barrier to success; it's a bridge. It can be the foundation upon which we build our most authentic and fulfilling lives but only if we're willing to do the work it takes to start our journey of healing.

In the pages ahead, you'll meet remarkable individuals who have faced profound adversity in both childhood and/or adulthood and emerged stronger. Their stories are a testament to the power of the human spirit, offering inspiration and practical lessons for moving forward. You'll also discover actionable tools to help you better understand how trauma has shaped your own life and career and how you can take back control.

Although many of the stories you'll read stem from childhood experiences, not all trauma begins early in life. Some stories will reflect how a short but intensely painful period can reverberate across decades if left unaddressed.

Trauma is not bound by age, timeline, or category. What matters most is how we confront it, process it, and choose to move forward.

Whether you're leading a company, a team, a classroom, a home, or simply your own life, unaddressed trauma can quietly shape your decisions, relationships, and performance. Left unchecked, it can have devastating consequences not only for you but also for those who love and rely on you.

Your story isn't finished yet. The next chapter of your life is still being written—and *Dealing with Healing* is here to help you write it with clarity, courage, and purpose. If this book helps even one person take the next step toward healing, then my goal has been accomplished.

CHAPTER 1

# From Caregiver to Changemaker: Nursing, Entrepreneurship, and Healing Housing

Growing up in a small town, I was raised by two remarkable individuals who became my first examples of what it means to serve others. My mother was a gentle homemaker with a talent for creating warmth and stability, whereas my father, a dedicated general surgeon, devoted his life to healing others. Their lives revolved around service, and watching them inspired me to follow in their footsteps. From an early age, I knew I was drawn to the art of caregiving.

At fourteen, I began volunteering as a candy striper at a local nursing home. From the moment I stepped into those bustling corridors filled with the sharp scent of antiseptic and the rhythmic hum of medical monitors, I felt an undeniable pull toward nursing. I wasn't only delivering meals or folding laundry; I was connecting with people during some of the most vulnerable moments of their lives. By sixteen, I was working at the local hospital, learning firsthand the power of presence and compassion in the face of hardship. I felt deeply fulfilled and knew I was exactly where I was meant to be. Nursing school was a natural next step.

During nursing school, I explored clinical rotations, but it was the surgical intensive care unit at Vanderbilt University where I truly found my calling. The fast-paced, high-stakes environment was exhilarating.

I thrived on the adrenaline, caring for critically ill postsurgical patients and acute trauma victims. Each shift was unpredictable and demanding, but I loved every moment of it.

Working with trauma patients exposed me to the harsh realities of life and loss. Every day, I worked with patients suffering from gunshot wounds, car accidents, and severe injuries. The intensity of the work required not only medical expertise but also emotional resilience. Communicating with families who received devastating news taught me invaluable lessons about empathy and the human spirit.

One night, after a particularly grueling shift, I sat with a mother who had lost her son in a car accident. Her grief was palpable, and in that moment, I realized the profound impact of simply being present for someone in their darkest hour.

During my early career, I also worked part-time at the city hospital's emergency room, which was known in the community as the "knife and gun club." Here, I encountered the poorest of the poor, the unhoused, and those struggling with addiction. This experience deepened my commitment to serving those in need. The stories I heard and the people I met reinforced my belief in the importance of providing care and support to society's most vulnerable.

After several years, I transitioned to working with Tennessee Donor Services, the local organ donor agency. This role brought new emotional challenges.

At twenty-six, I was approaching families who had been told their loved one was brain-dead, asking if they would consider organ donation. It was an incredibly difficult conversation to have, but also a deeply meaningful one. Yet, it was also rewarding to facilitate the gift of life for others. Families who, in their darkest moments, found solace in knowing their loved ones' organs would help save others taught me lessons in courage I'll never forget. Their generosity has left an indelible impression on me.

After years of navigating the intensity of nursing, I stepped away from the profession to focus on raising my two children. Although I cherished this time at home, I couldn't ignore the entrepreneurial spark within me. I began teaching myself calligraphy and addressing wedding invitations as a creative outlet. I also designed and sold hand-monogrammed stationery to brides who needed wedding stationery and hostess gifts. Before long, I noticed a gap in the market for personalized stationery and gifts, and what started as a hobby quickly evolved into a thriving business.

Over the next fifteen years, I built a multimillion-dollar manufacturing and wholesaling company, creating products sold in more than 1,200 retail stores nationwide. The journey was a whirlwind of late nights, tough decisions, and balancing motherhood with business ownership. It was far from easy, but it taught me invaluable lessons about staying strong, adaptability, and the power of pursuing a vision.

But success is rarely a straight line. The economic crash of 2008 led to the closure of many retail stores, and by 2010, I made the difficult decision to close my company.

I spent the next several years doing consulting and accounting for a medical company, and it was during this period that I was pulled into a giving-back opportunity—one that would change the course of my life.

I began volunteering with a teaching program at the Tennessee Prison for Women, where I taught an eight-week course to incarcerated women on decision-making. I didn't know what to expect when I first walked through those prison gates, but I quickly realized this was no ordinary classroom. The women I worked with weren't only learning about decision-making—they were confronting the weight of past choices, the lasting fallout of trauma, and the overwhelming challenge of starting over.

On my third eight-week session, I was paired with Stacey, an inmate whose story stayed with me long after I left the prison. She had endured childhood sexual abuse, lived on the streets, battled addiction, and cycled in and out of jail. But what struck me wasn't what she had been through; it was her unrelenting determination to build something better.

Stacey was getting out soon. She wanted to start fresh in Nashville, far from the people and patterns that had pulled her down in the past. But she had nothing—no family to turn to, no money, and no stable place to go. She had done the hard work of getting sober, but without a safe environment, the odds were stacked against her.

So, I started researching. Surely, there had to be resources for women like Stacey, those who had completed treatment and were committed to recovery but needed a real chance at stability. I searched for transitional programs, affordable housing, recovery support ... anything.

What I found was devastatingly inadequate.

There were some shelters, but many had wait-lists or time limits. There were halfway houses, but they often lacked structured recovery programs. Nearly everything required some form of financial security—something women coming straight out of incarceration or treatment rarely had. I kept thinking:

"How can we expect these women to rebuild their lives if we don't give them the space and opportunity to build their own foundation?"

That question wouldn't leave me. I knew I had to do something. And so, the seeds for Healing Housing were planted.

As luck (or God) would have it, the church I attend, Brentwood United Methodist Church in Brentwood, TN, is a Certified Recovery Church. For years, our church had a dedicated meeting space in which the community could hold multiple AA recovery meetings and other recovery-related activities. Knowing that the church had already built a base of support for those in recovery, I approached my pastor and childhood friend, Reverend Davis Chappell. I shared with him my prison volunteer experience and the gnawing feeling it had left behind. I shared Stacey's story with him and my desire to do something meaningful for women like Stacey—those in early recovery who complete treatment but exit their program with no financial resources and no safe place to land to continue their recovery.

Of course, with no strong support system, the cycle repeats itself as these women inevitably go back to their familiar haunts and pick up their old coping patterns of drug and alcohol use. This cycle repeats itself mindlessly over and over again, leaving in its wake not only a huge cost to the women but their families and society at large.

With the assistance of Davis and several other staff pastors, I was introduced one by one to women in the church who showed interest in working on this "seed of an idea" with me. We started with nothing other than an intense desire to serve this underserved population of women. We committed to meeting every week to work on breathing life into this vision. Each woman brought a unique set of gifts and talents to bear.

We weren't experts, and we certainly had no idea what we were doing at first, but we had a vision and a passion to serve, and that was enough to get us started. Our team spent two years developing our vision into what would become Healing Housing—a transitional living facility for women in recovery who have no financial resources and no safe and structured environment in which to continue their recovery work.

With the generosity and prayers of many donors who believed in our vision, Healing Housing opened its doors in April 2017. Women receive housing for the first twelve weeks at no cost, followed by a modest fee, most of which is returned to them upon successful completion of the program. But more than a place to stay, it has become a home where love lives and a space where women regain their footing, build accountability, and step into a new chapter of their lives with stability and purpose. The women state that the individual as well as group therapy they receive while in our program has allowed them to begin to deal with their healing and write their new stories each and every day.

We started Healing Housing to solve a problem for a specific group of women—those who had completed treatment and were on the brink of homelessness, rebuilding their lives after addiction. The more I listened and learned from the stories of our women, the more my perceptions of addiction shifted. The way I used to view and, quite frankly, judge "the alcoholic over there," the more I realized that Healing Housing wasn't housing addicts; it was housing big-T ***Trauma Survivors***. I finally connected the dots. You don't wake up at sixteen and decide to become a drug addict or an alcoholic. That's not what happens. Many factors are at play that start a downward spiral, and childhood trauma looms as the largest contributing factor.

I fully expected to see a transformation in the women we served. What I did not expect was the profound effect Healing Housing would have on the broader community.

In the beginning, I served as the program's executive director. As we gained traction, people from all walks of life—donors, volunteers, business leaders, and neighbors—reached out. Along with offering financial support and resources, they began sharing something even more personal: their own stories.

I started receiving emails and handwritten letters and having personal conversations filled with stories of trauma and deep pain. The people sharing privately with me would often say that this was the first time they had ever spoken openly about their trauma before. Men and women, successful professionals, parents, and educators would pull me aside after a fundraiser or educational event and share:

> *"My brother struggled with addiction for years, and I never knew how to help. He died recently. He never got over what happened to him as a child. He never would agree to get help.*

*It broke our family into pieces. We all suffered as a result of his unresolved trauma."*

*"My mother's drinking shaped my entire childhood. I never talk about it, but I see now how it still impacts me."*

*"I've always been the high achiever, but deep down, I've been running from my childhood sexual trauma."*

These stories weren't coming from women in the program; they were coming from the people supporting it. These were "regular" people—functioning members of society, professionals with successful careers, parents raising families. Yet, their stories made one thing clear: The wounds of trauma and addiction weren't isolated to those in jails, treatment centers, or recovery programs. People who are wounded by deep trauma were hiding in plain sight, woven into the fabric of our communities, often obscured beneath layers of success, resilience, silence, and shame.

That realization changed everything for me.

Trauma survivors aren't "those people over there"; they are some of the people closest to us. They are our neighbors, church friends, family members, and coworkers. Trauma survivors are silently suffering everywhere. There are those who have found a path of healing, but there are many others who are desperately coexisting with their unresolved trauma. Trauma knows no socioeconomic or gender boundaries.

Trauma manifests in different, sometimes unusual ways. For some, it leads to substance abuse. For others, it leads to perfectionism, overworking, chronic stress, or failed relationships. It might look like aptitude on the outside, but for many who live with unresolved trauma, it feels like an invisible weight that will never be lifted.

This wave of personal confessions, from people I least expected, was an awakening for me. It was a mirror, reflecting back to the community the reality that trauma is far more widespread and often deeply hidden than we realize. Founding Healing Housing was certainly an effort to offer help to the most vulnerable who had fallen into the crushing arms of addiction to numb the pain from their debilitating trauma.

But what about the masses of walking wounded, those silently suffering with their unresolved trauma but who escaped the path of addiction? Many of them were sharing their stories of trauma with me. Not surprisingly, many of them were highly successful executives in the business community. As an entrepreneur and business leader, I was amazed at the success most of these individuals had achieved despite their significant history of trauma. I was also amazed at the fact that many of them had never spoken about it or received any therapy or other help to address what had happened. They had simply gutted it out and worked their fingers to the bone hoping the pain and shame would eventually fade. But of course, this approach rarely succeeds.

*How and where do they find their relief?*

It was this question that haunted me. That's when I knew I had to write this book.

I had spent years working in trauma care, emergency rooms, and most recently, recovery spaces, yet this was the first time I fully grasped how deeply trauma was woven into everyday life. This book was born from the realization that if we don't talk about trauma, if we don't name it, process it, and heal from it, it will continue to shape our lives in ways we don't recognize.

Healing Housing taught me that trauma has a universal reach. If you haven't been directly touched by big-T Trauma, I can assure you that someone close to you has. According to research published in *Harvard Business Review,* six in ten men and five in ten women will experience at least one trauma in their lifetime, and roughly 6 percent will develop posttraumatic stress disorder (PTSD). These numbers show up in boardrooms, classrooms, and leadership roles every day.

For many high-achieving professionals, unresolved trauma may look like hidden anxiety, strained relationships, or burnout. Left unaddressed, it can quietly undermine both personal health and organizational performance. If we want to truly heal, both individually and as a society, we need to start openly acknowledging it.

This is the book I wish every person who ever shared their stories of unaddressed trauma with me had been able to read. The business leaders who shared their stories with me were determined that sharing their personal stories of trauma and healing would help open the conversation to a wider audience. Their stories would be an acknowledgment that you are not alone. You may be suffering silently, but you are not alone. You, too, can find relief from the burdens you've been carrying.

The goal of this book isn't to prescribe a single route to healing; it's about fostering a deeper understanding. Through research, personal stories, and reflections, it explores how trauma influences both our personal lives and professional trajectories. Rather than offering a one-size-fits-all solution, it encourages self-awareness, helping you identify patterns, recognize their effects, and explore pathways to healing that align with your own experiences.

## Throughout these pages, you will:

- Gain a deeper understanding of trauma; how it manifests mentally, physically, and emotionally; and how it may be shaping your relationships, decisions, and career trajectory, sometimes driving success but other times triggering self-doubt and setbacks.

- Examine insights from the ACE study and learn how early-life adversity can have lasting effects and why acknowledging these connections is a powerful step toward change.

- Gain perspective from an experienced clinician who explains how trauma shows up in leaders and workplaces and why addressing it is essential not only for individual well-being but also for organizational health.

- Read real stories from high-performing professionals who have faced profound challenges in childhood and adulthood and found ways to reclaim their lives and careers—not only surviving but growing and thriving.

- Explore new perspectives that challenge traditional narratives about trauma, offering fresh ways to reframe experiences and move forward with clarity and confidence.

- Engage in reflection with thought-provoking questions and prompts at the end of key chapters to help you apply these insights in a personal and meaningful way. Some may feel familiar, but as you read and work through this book, you may find that your answers shift, deepen, and grow as you become more comfortable with the idea of dealing with your healing.

By the time you reach the final pages, my hope is that you will not only understand how trauma can affect one's past but also how it can empower you to take ownership of your future. Healing isn't about erasing what's come before. It's about facing it, dealing with it, finding peace, and stepping forward with intention.

As a business leader, you have a responsibility to lead others. Leading with unaddressed trauma lurking in your background can have devastating consequences on you and those you lead and negative consequences for your business's bottom line.

CHAPTER 2

# The Ripple Effect of Trauma in Shaping Our Lives and Careers

Trauma is a part of life that touches nearly everyone in some shape or form, yet it often hides in plain sight. We tend to think of trauma as something catastrophic—an accident, a tragedy, or an act of violence. But trauma also resides in the quieter, cumulative experiences that erode our sense of safety and self-worth over time. Whether we recognize it or not, trauma shapes the way we move through the world, affecting how we show up in relationships, how we manage stress, and how we navigate our careers.

Through my work with Healing Housing, I saw trauma's influence firsthand—not only in the women we served but in the many professionals, volunteers, and donors who shared their own untold stories with me. What started as an effort to help women in recovery turned into a broader realization: Trauma isn't confined to one group of people; it affects nearly everyone, often in ways we don't acknowledge.

I began to notice patterns. Some people struggled with addiction. Others threw themselves into work, overachieving to prove their worth. Some found themselves stuck in toxic relationships, whereas others avoided connection altogether. The trauma didn't manifest in obvious ways, it hid beneath perfectionism, chronic stress, and even outward success.

This realization changed the way I thought about healing. Trauma is not something to "get over"—it shapes our behaviors, choices, and even careers. If we don't recognize its lasting mark, we can end up repeating cycles that hold us back.

Understanding trauma, its origins, different forms, and how it impacts our lives is an essential step toward breaking free. It's not about dwelling on the past; it's about giving ourselves the tools to move forward with clarity and strength.

## Understanding Big-T and Little-t Trauma

Trauma is more than an unpleasant experience. It's an event—or a series of events—that overwhelms your ability to cope. It leaves you feeling powerless, shaken, and unable to return to a sense of normalcy. Importantly, trauma is subjective; what deeply affects one person may not affect another in the same way.

For the purposes of this book, we distinguish between "big-T" and "little-t" trauma.

# Different Types of Trauma

| Type of Trauma | Description | Examples |
|---|---|---|
| "Big T" Trauma | Major, life-altering events that are typically recognized as traumatic | Natural disasters, physical or sexual assault, witnessing a violent crime, severe injury, sudden death of a loved one, pregnancy loss, or abortion |
| "Little t" Trauma | Smaller, cumulative stressors that may not seem traumatic on the surface but have a lasting impact over time | Persistent criticism from a parent, teacher, or boss, emotional neglect, chronic financial instability, feeling excluded, microaggressions and relationship betrayals |
| Chronic Trauma | Ongoing exposure to distressing circumstances that erodes emotional resilience | Growing up in an abusive home, long-term workplace harassment, repeated bullying, racism, sexism and enduring other forms of systemic discrimination |
| Complex Trauma | A combination of multiple, interwoven traumatic experiences, often starting in childhood | A child raised in a home with substance abuse, neglect, sexual abuse, or repeated emotional abuse, cycles of abandonment or instability |

What makes little-t traumas so dangerous is their cumulative effect. A single instance of being overlooked at work may not seem traumatic. However, if that experience echoes past wounds—such as being ignored as a child, feeling unseen in school, or being repeatedly dismissed—it can reinforce a deeper belief that you don't matter.

Understanding trauma in all its forms allows us to recognize its presence in our lives, not as a way to define ourselves but to reclaim our story so we can write a new one.

## The Lasting Effects of Trauma on Identity

Trauma isn't only something that happened in the past; it fundamentally shapes how we see ourselves, how we relate to others, and how we move through the world. Its effects often surface in subtle but powerful ways, particularly in our professional lives, where unprocessed wounds can influence everything from confidence and ambition to leadership style and decision-making.

Mentally, trauma disrupts cognitive processes like concentration, memory, and decision-making. Even small stressors can feel overwhelming, triggering a fight-or-flight response that makes it difficult to think clearly. Have you ever found yourself spiraling over a minor critique or hesitating when faced with a big decision? Trauma often lies at the root of these reactions, interfering with your ability to trust your instincts or focus on the task at hand.

Emotionally, trauma can feel like carrying a weight you can't set down. It floods your nervous system with feelings of fear, anger, shame, or sadness that may be difficult to process. These emotions might surface as intense outbursts, or they might hide behind emotional numbness, making it hard to engage in meaningful relationships or even recognize your own feelings. Over time, this emotional turbulence creates barriers that limit trust, communication, and connection.

Physically, trauma embeds itself in the body. Chronic pain, tension headaches, digestive issues, and fatigue are common symptoms reported by those suffering from unresolved trauma. It's not unusual for survivors to feel like their bodies are betraying them, when in reality, their bodies are carrying the weight of unprocessed emotions.

In high-stakes professional environments, these effects can become even more pronounced. Trauma can make it difficult to handle feedback, form trusting relationships with colleagues, or advocate for yourself in leadership positions. It may manifest as perfectionism—pushing yourself to the brink in an attempt to avoid criticism—or self-sabotage, hesitating to take risks out of fear of failure.

Unprocessed trauma isn't confined to personal experiences—it can also develop in professional environments in ways we often underestimate. Persistent, hostile behavior from colleagues or superior workplace bullying can create a toxic environment, gradually chipping away at your sense of self-worth and confidence. Over time, this stress can lead to isolation, chronic anxiety, or burnout.

For many, workplace trauma isn't as overt as bullying or harassment. It's the accumulation of being overlooked for promotions, experiencing microaggressions, or working in a high-pressure culture where unrealistic expectations and fear of failure dominate.

These experiences don't affect individuals alone; they ripple outward, influencing team dynamics, workplace culture, and even entire organizations. When professionals carry the weight of trauma into leadership roles, it can shape the company's values, decision-making processes, and overall well-being of the team. Recognizing these patterns in ourselves and our workplaces is the first step in creating environments that support growth, empowerment, and healing.

## Understanding Trauma's Influence on Professional Life

Through my work, I've learned that many struggles professionals face today don't start in the workplace. The fears, insecurities, and stressors that show up in adulthood often have roots in early-life experiences. For a bit more context in helping us understand the true consequences of traumatic childhood events, we will examine the Adverse Childhood Experiences (ACE) Study, a groundbreaking research project that connects early trauma to long-term health outcomes in adults.

The ACE study confirmed what I had already begun to suspect: The challenges people face in their careers, relationships, and mental health are often tied to experiences from years, even decades, earlier.

But how does childhood trauma continue to shape our adult lives? What does the research tell us about the long-term effects of adversity?

In the next chapter, we'll review the ACE study in more detail and explore what it reveals about the connection between trauma and professional life. We'll also discuss how knowing your own ACE score can provide insight into the challenges you face today.

Healing isn't about looking back. It's about understanding our past, so we can step fully into our future.

CHAPTER 3

# The ACE Study: How Childhood Trauma Shapes Health and Careers

All these experiences, the women I worked with in recovery, the community members who quietly shared or kept their stories hidden, and the patterns I noticed across countless conversations and careers led me to a pivotal realization. Many of the challenges adults face in their lives and careers don't begin in adulthood. The shame, burnout, anxiety, and self-sabotage we carry into the boardroom, kitchen, or therapist's office often have roots that run far deeper than we imagine.

This realization compelled me to step back and dig deeper. I wanted to understand what the research said about the long-term ramifications of trauma. What I discovered stopped me in my tracks.

## A Groundbreaking Framework for Understanding Trauma

The Adverse Childhood Experiences (ACE) study, now considered one of the most important public health studies ever conducted, provided validation and clear language for something countless people had intuitively sensed but never had words to describe. Conducted in the late 1990s by the Centers for Disease Control and Prevention (CDC) and Kaiser Permanente, the study had its surprising origins in an obesity clinic run by Dr. Vincent Felitti. In the 1980s, Dr. Felitti was perplexed by a troubling pattern: More than half of his clinic's participants dropped out of his weight loss program despite having successfully lost significant amounts of weight. Determined to understand why, he began in-depth interviews with former participants. He discovered an unexpected common thread—many had experienced childhood sexual abuse and other severe traumas. Further investigation revealed that, for these patients, excessive weight gain often served as psychological protection, a shield against painful memories or unwanted attention. This astonishing insight prompted a collaboration with Dr. Robert Anda from the CDC, ultimately leading to the expansive ACE study.

The ACE study surveyed more than 17,000 adults from diverse backgrounds, investigating how childhood trauma and adversity affected their long-term physical, emotional, and professional health. Notably, the study wasn't focused solely on severe or widely recognized traumatic events. Instead, it examined quieter, less visible burdens—hidden experiences children carry when their home environments are unpredictable, unsupportive, or unsafe. This included emotional neglect, physical or emotional abuse, and household dysfunction related to parental mental illness, substance abuse, domestic violence, incarceration, or parental separation and divorce.

Researchers identified ten common forms of adversity that children frequently encounter, grouped into three main categories:

1. **Abuse:** physical, emotional, and sexual abuse

2. **Neglect:** physical and emotional neglect

3. **Household Dysfunction:** growing up with a parent struggling with substance abuse, mental illness, experiencing parental separation or divorce, witnessing domestic violence, or having a family member incarcerated

## Lifetime Repercussions of ACE: The Body Remembers

One of the most powerful insights from the ACE study was how clearly it demonstrated the physical and emotional effects of childhood trauma. The trauma we experience doesn't simply fade away. It lives on, biologically embedded within our nervous systems, influencing our physical and emotional health far into adulthood.

The statistics from the ACE study are sobering. Individuals with an ACE score of four or more face significantly increased risks for serious health issues and emotional challenges. Hard-to-treat conditions like chronic migraines, autoimmune disorders, persistent fatigue, anxiety, digestive issues, and ongoing pain can be the body's way of signaling the lasting imprint of unresolved trauma.

To put this into perspective, *Mandated Reporter* has noted that the CDC estimates each individual survivor of child maltreatment incurs an average lifetime cost of approximately $210,012. These substantial financial burdens highlight the often-unseen ways trauma reshapes a person's life and extends into society. Child maltreatment is linked not only to immediate physical harm but also to long-term emotional and behavioral issues, including increased risks of aggression, anxiety, depression, conduct disorders, substance abuse, intimate partner violence, and suicide. What begins in families eventually reaches classrooms, clinics, courtrooms, and workplaces, straining every system that supports community well-being.

# Lifetime Repercussions of ACEs

| People with an ACE Score of 4 or MORE have an increased risk for: | |
|---|---|
| Suicide | 1550% |
| COPD | 400% |
| Loss of Vision | 400% |
| Heart Attack | 275% |
| Kidney Disease | 275% |
| Heart Disease | 250% |
| Arthritis | 250% |
| Strokes | 250% |
| Diabetes | 200% |
| Cancer | 150% |
| | |
| Attempted Suicide | 12X |
| Likely to be Alcoholics | 7X |
| Had sex before age 15 | 6X |
| Cancer or Heart Disease | 2X |
| Likely to Smoke | 2X |
| | |
| **Men with ACEs of 6 or higher** | |
| More likely to have injected drugs than men with no history of ACEs | 46X |
| Much more likely to have chronic health issues | 46X |
| Exceedingly high predictability of needing mental health treatment | 46X |

# Adverse Childhood Experiences (ACE) Questionnaire

**Instructions:** Below is a list of 10 categories of Adverse Childhood Experiences (ACEs). From the list below, place a checkmark next to each ACE category that you experienced prior to your 18th birthday. Then add up the number of ACEs you experienced and put the total number at the bottom.

1. Did you feel that you didn't have enough to eat, had to wear dirty clothes or had no one to protect you or take care of you? ☐
2. Did you lose a parent through divorce, abandonment, death or other reason? ☐
3. Did you live with anyone who was depressed, mentally ill, or attempted suicide? ☐
4. Did you live with anyone who had a problem with drinking or using drugs, including prescription drugs? ☐
5. Did your parents or adults in your home ever hit, punch, beat, or threaten to harm each other? ☐
6. Did you live with anyone who went to jail or prison? ☐
7. Did a parent or adult in your home ever swear at you, insult you or put you down? ☐
8. Did a parent or adult in your home ever hit, beat, kick, or physically hurt you in any way? ☐
9. Did you feel that no one in your family loved you or thought you were special? ☐
10. Did you experience unwanted sexual contact (such as fondling or oral/anal/vaginal intercourse/penetration)? ☐

**Your ACE score is the total number of checked responses** ☐

## These statistics illustrate the increased health risks for individuals with an ACE score of four or more:

***Source**: Felitti, V. J., Anda, R. F., Nordenberg, D., Williamson, D. F., Spitz, A. M., Edwards, V., Koss, M. P., & Marks, J. S. (1998). Relationship of Childhood Abuse and Household Dysfunction to Many of the Leading Causes of Death in Adults: The Adverse Childhood Experiences (ACE) Study. American Journal of Preventive Medicine, 14(4), 245–258.*

Look around at your workplace, on your commute, and in your community. The people represented by these numbers are coworkers, neighbors, and parents simply trying their best to manage daily life while carrying unseen burdens.

When I first encountered these findings, I immediately thought of the women I worked with at Healing Housing and the professionals who would quietly share their struggles after workshops or speaking events. Again and again, they voiced the same uncertainty: *"I don't know why I'm like this."*

The reasons behind those patterns came into clearer focus. Experiences from our childhood, whether at age five, ten, or fifteen, can leave lasting marks that shape how we handle stress, accept feedback, trust others, and either step confidently into leadership or shrink away from it.

This is why the ACE framework is so powerful in both the workplace and the home. It isn't about looking back simply to revisit the past; it's about uncovering what drives us today. With clarity about the roots of our behaviors, we gain insight that makes healing possible, and with that healing, we can choose to write a different story for our future.

## Your Turn: Take the ACE Questionnaire

Let's pause here. Before moving forward, I want to offer you the same reflective opportunity that the ACE study participants had: a chance to look at your own early experiences and consider how they might be shaping your life today.

This isn't a test. It's not a diagnostic tool. It's simply an invitation to explore honestly and compassionately what might have influenced your current patterns, behaviors, and beliefs.

Take your time with the questionnaire below. For each question, answer yes or no. Each yes answer counts as one point toward your ACE score.

## Adverse Childhood Experiences (ACE) Questionnaire

Your ACE score is the total number of yes answers. That's it. Simple but not always easy.

***Source***: *Adverse Childhood Experiences (ACE) Questionnaire for Adults. California Surgeon General's Advisory Committee, Office of the California Surgeon General.*

For some, this exercise might bring clarity or validation. For others, it may stir emotions or memories long buried. Both reactions are completely natural. If your ACE score is high, I want you to hear clearly: You aren't broken. Your experiences make sense. You're not alone.

If your score is below four or even zero, that doesn't mean you haven't faced hardship. Some forms of trauma aren't captured in this questionnaire. Emotional wounds from chronic stress, grief, cultural expectations, or subtle exclusion still deeply matter.

What about the traumas that don't fit neatly into these categories—the ones people carry silently—the traumas that go unspoken but create emotional havoc due to the immense guilt, shame, and fear of judgment they carry? Trauma can also be compounded by personal and cultural expectations, making healing even more complex.

The ACE questionnaire is only one lens, one doorway into deeper reflection about how we carry what we've been through and how we might begin to carry it differently.

## When Trauma Follows Us into the Workplace

As we've explored, trauma's fallout isn't confined to physical or emotional health alone. It quietly shapes our professional lives, careers, and daily interactions at work in profound yet subtle ways. Many of us don't recognize these patterns as trauma driven, yet they significantly influence how we engage professionally, affecting our confidence, decision-making, and interpersonal relationships.

The ACE study clearly demonstrated that childhood adversity and trauma create lasting impacts on our nervous systems. Those consequences can influence our stress responses, emotional regulation, and even our fundamental beliefs about ourselves and others. These adaptations, initially protective and necessary for survival, become limiting when carried forward into our adult professional lives.

## In professional settings, trauma-driven behaviors can appear as the following:

- **Perfectionism:** Working relentlessly and tirelessly, driven by an underlying fear of criticism, rejection, or failure. Individuals who experienced intense criticism, instability, or conditional love in childhood might develop perfectionist tendencies, believing they must excel to maintain acceptance or approval.

- **Avoidance:** Hesitating to step into leadership roles, avoiding constructive criticism, or steering clear of challenging tasks due to fears rooted in past experiences. Childhood trauma involving judgment or repeated failure can make professional risk-taking feel disproportionately threatening in adulthood.

- **People-pleasing:** Routinely overcommitting, saying yes to every request, even at great personal cost. This pattern often emerges in individuals who learned in childhood to prioritize others' needs above their own in an effort to avoid conflict or secure emotional safety.

- **Trust Issues:** Difficulty trusting supervisors, colleagues, or even oneself. Experiences of betrayal, neglect, or instability in childhood relationships can foster ongoing difficulty in building genuine connections at work or fully integrating into professional teams.

These responses are not signs of personal shortcomings or professional inadequacy. Rather, they are understandable adaptations—learned behaviors from difficult childhood environments that helped individuals survive emotionally. Recognizing these adaptations for what they truly are is the first essential step toward healing and professional growth.

## Consider these professional scenarios illustrating how trauma can subtly shape our behaviors at work:

- **Difficulty Trusting Colleagues and Supervisors:** A professional who grew up in a household marked by emotional neglect or instability might find it difficult to trust coworkers, supervisors, or mentors. In meetings, they may be hesitant to speak up, constantly fearing judgment or exploitation. Even neutral interactions can feel threatening. They might isolate themselves, limiting their professional growth and the possibility of meaningful collaboration.

- **Overreacting to Constructive Feedback:** A professional who experienced childhood verbal abuse might struggle significantly with accepting constructive criticism as an adult. Even gentle feedback might trigger feelings of inadequacy, rejection, or fear of failure, causing emotional withdrawal or defensive reactions. These strong responses can stall career growth, hinder professional relationships, and create barriers to continuous learning and development.

- **Driven by Unconscious Need to Prove Worth:** A high-achieving executive whose childhood trauma left them feeling devoid of self-worth or whose self-worth was developed based on achievements may demonstrate a relentless work ethic and continuous productivity but may be privately plagued by an unconscious fear that their value hinges solely on their performance. They may struggle to take breaks, delegate, or set boundaries, fearing that slowing down will expose their perceived inadequacies or result in rejection.

These scenarios demonstrate how deeply childhood experiences can shape professional behaviors. By seeing these behaviors as protective adaptations rather than personal failings, we can better understand ourselves and others and take intentional steps toward healthier professional lives.

## Reflection: Connecting Childhood Experiences to Current Behaviors

Let's pause here to consider how these patterns might appear in your own professional life. Take a moment to reflect on these questions, approaching them with honesty, compassion, and curiosity. Write your answers or simply think about them:

- ***Are there recurring professional behaviors or patterns in my life that seem difficult to explain logically?***

________________________________________

________________________________________

________________________________________

________________________________________

- ***Do I notice a strong emotional reaction to feedback, perceived criticism, or professional risks that might connect to my early experiences?***

________________________________________

________________________________________

________________________________________

________________________________________

- ***Have I observed patterns of perfectionism, avoidance, or people-pleasing that seem resistant to change?***

______________________________________________

______________________________________________

______________________________________________

______________________________________________

- ***How might my professional relationships change if I approached them with greater awareness and compassion toward my past?***

______________________________________________

______________________________________________

______________________________________________

______________________________________________

These reflections aren't intended to trigger judgment or shame. Rather, they offer a pathway toward greater clarity and the opportunity to begin reshaping old narratives in a healthier, more empowered direction.

## Beyond Awareness: Moving Toward Healing

The ACE framework is powerful precisely because it transforms confusion into clarity. But awareness alone is only the beginning. True healing and change come from the decisions and actions that follow awareness.

As you begin recognizing how your past experiences might shape your professional and personal behaviors, internally consider these questions on how you can gently and intentionally move forward:

- How can you create safe spaces, both personally and professionally, to begin practicing trust, boundaries, and self-compassion?

- Can you identify a trusted colleague, mentor, or therapist with whom you can safely explore these insights and begin reframing old patterns?

- In moments of stress or emotional intensity at work, can you pause briefly to consider whether your response might be rooted in old wounds and then consciously choose a different path forward?

The ultimate goal isn't simply to acknowledge your past but to cultivate the capacity to move beyond it. Healing involves gradually rewriting old narratives into stories of strength and empowerment. It's not about erasing or denying pain but integrating your experiences in a way that allows for growth, wisdom, and a deeper connection to your own humanity.

As we continue through this book, you will encounter real stories of successful business leaders who've recognized the connections between childhood experiences and their adult lives. You'll see clearly how people with a variety of ACE scores, ranging from milder to more significant trauma, have successfully reshaped their professional identities and personal lives to write a new story.

These are stories of genuine healing and growth. You'll witness transformations happening through leadership, mentorship, community involvement, therapy, and everyday personal decisions. You'll see that no matter how complex or challenging your starting point is, change is always possible.

This is perhaps the most powerful lesson of all: Your past experiences, no matter how significant, challenging, or complicated, do not have the final say in your professional or personal future. Recognizing the connections between past adversity and present challenges isn't a sentence; it's an invitation. It's an invitation to deeper self-awareness, understanding, self-compassion, and ultimately, profound growth.

## You Are Exactly Where You Need to Be

Before we move on, take a moment here to ground yourself. Take a deep breath. Acknowledge the courage and strength it takes to explore these truths about yourself.

## Remember this clearly:

- You're not behind.
- You're not too late.
- You're exactly where you need to be right now: reading, reflecting, and gently opening yourself to new ideas.

This awareness is a powerful first step. From here, you get to decide what comes next.

Your past doesn't get the last word—*you* do.

Let's keep going.

CHAPTER 4

# DISC: Understanding Behavioral Styles for Better Connection

In my first session with a new business consulting or coaching client, I always ask if they are actively in therapy or have ever had therapy. Many of my clients are in active therapy. The coaching relationship serves a different purpose than therapy, and it's important that the client understands those differences. Coaching focuses on the present and how to move forward, whereas therapy has a much broader focus on past events. As we've learned so far, these experiences from the past can certainly inform the present.

For this reason, I ask clients to take the ACE questionnaire and a DISC behavioral assessment. Most of my clients have never heard of the ACE questionnaire, and many have never taken a behavioral assessment. Coincidentally or not, most of my clients have an ACE score of four or greater. Typically, their therapist will work with them to address traumatic issues from the past. My role is to keep the clients' focus on the here and now, so they can navigate their daily lives in a productive manner even as they do the necessary work to heal past hurts.

When we think about healing from trauma, our minds often go straight to the past, the pain, the events, the impact. But healing isn't only about where we've been; it's also about how we show up now in our relationships, our communication, and the way we carry ourselves through the world.

Whereas our ACE score provides a lens through which we can view our past, having a lens through which we can view ourselves in the present moment can also be extremely helpful. That's where taking a deep dive into our behavioral patterns becomes incredibly enlightening. The DISC assessment provides great insight "behind the curtain" of the emotions that are driving our needs-based behaviors.

You might be wondering: *What does a behavioral assessment have to do with trauma recovery?*

For so many of the people I've worked with, the answer is: everything.

When we experience trauma, especially early in life, it can shape the way we communicate, relate, and protect ourselves. Some of us become hyper independent. Others avoid conflict at all costs. Still others push themselves relentlessly, always trying to prove they're good enough. These behaviors often begin as survival strategies, but over time, they can keep us stuck.

The DISC behavioral assessment is a tool that offers us a practical way to understand our behavior within a predictable framework. It gives us language for identifying our behavioral patterns and insights into how those patterns serve or sabotage us in our daily lives. When reviewed with a trained DISC professional, the results can become a powerful companion in the healing process. Understanding the power of self-awareness and how it impacts our personal and professional lives can be a catalyst for needed behavioral shifts.

When the lightbulb of self-awareness clicks on, we can shed old patterns born out of trauma—patterns that no longer serve us—and learn new behavioral patterns that will benefit us in all our important relationships, whether business or personal. I have personally seen clients transform how they lead their organizations by combining insights from their ACE score and DISC debrief with a committed effort to build their self-awareness muscles. They transform not only themselves but their entire organization.

In every story that follows in this book, you'll see the participant's *Natural DISC Style* listed in the "Interview Dossier." When we understand our behavioral style and the styles of those around us, we gain access to better relationships, healthier workplaces, and a deeper sense of agency in our healing journey.

## DISC Deconstructed

DISC is a behavioral tool that helps explain how you tend to behave across different environments, especially under pressure. Completing the assessment is easy. I send clients a link to the assessment, which they can complete in about fifteen minutes. I receive the results and then schedule the "results debrief session" with the client.

During the debrief, I guide participants through a comprehensive review of the DISC model and explain the meaning of their individual results. I offer this training to both corporate teams and individual executives, and almost without fail, someone asks, "Can trauma affect my results?" The answer is a resounding yes.

Below, you will find highlights from the DISC training that will help you understand the model and how it applies to unlocking behavioral clues. Let's look at each style in brief, keeping in mind that most people are a blend of two or more styles. Taking the assessment and learning your *natural* and *adapted* DISC styles will give you clues as to how you move through the world.

## THE FOUR DISC STYLES:

- Dominant (D)
- Influencing (I)
- Steady (S)
- Conscientious (C)

### Dominant (D): The Driver

If you're a D, you're probably decisive, results-oriented, and not afraid to take charge. You like clarity, you move fast, and you'd rather fix a problem than talk about it for hours.

**What it looks like in action:** You get things done. You speak your mind. You're not here for fluff.

**What to watch for:** Ds can sometimes bulldoze people without meaning to. Slowing down and listening fully is a skill worth building.

### Influencing (I): The Connector

If you're an I, you're probably expressive, optimistic, and energized by people. You bring big energy into the room and often find yourself leading without even trying.

**What it looks like in action:** You motivate others, you love to collaborate, and you're great at building relationships.

**What to watch for:** Is can sometimes skim the surface or chase new ideas without follow-through. Learning to stay grounded and focused can help deepen both work and connection.

## Steady (S): The Anchor

If you're an S, you likely value harmony, reliability, and predictability. You're the calm in the storm and often the one people go to when they need grounding.

**What it looks like in action:** You're dependable, loyal, a good listener, and a team player.

**What to watch for:** Ss can avoid conflict to keep the peace and may struggle to speak up for their needs. Building assertiveness can be transformational.

## Conscientious (C): The Thinker

If you're a C, you're detail-oriented, analytical, and focused on getting things right. You like structure, data, and clear expectations.

**What it looks like in action:** You bring precision and care to your work. You ask the hard questions and do your homework.

**What to watch for:** Cs can get stuck in perfectionism or analysis paralysis. Learning to trust yourself—and others—can open new possibilities.

## Putting DISC into Practice

One of my recent clients stated:

*"Understanding DISC has helped me show up more fully—not just for others but also for myself. It's helped me make sense of how I used to over-function in relationships both personally and professionally. It's helped me lead with more compassion.* ***Most importantly, it's helped me hold space for people whose styles are radically different from mine."***

You don't need to be an expert to start applying DISC in your own life. What you need most is curiosity.

**Write out or simply think about your answers. Ask yourself:**

- ***Which DISC style feels most natural to me?***

____________________

____________________

____________________

____________________

- ***Where do I feel stuck, and could my behavioral patterns be part of that?***

____________________

____________________

____________________

____________________

- ***How might understanding others' styles help me feel less reactive, more connected, and more at peace?***

---

---

---

---

These questions are a starting point. As you work with them, you'll begin to see how tools like DISC and ACE provide structure for making sense of patterns that once felt confusing or overwhelming.

You will also notice that each trauma story in this book begins with an Interview Dossier. This includes the participant's ACE score, DISC natural style, and a few key life details. The goal is to give you a glimpse of how personality, environment, and lived experience intersect to shape patterns over time.

If you're curious about your own DISC profile, you'll find a link in the Resources section on page 177 to take the DISC assessment. In the notes section, add "I want to take the DISC assessment."

These are simply tools, ways of gaining deeper insight into who you are and how you move through the world. That awareness can help you make wiser choices, heal more fully, and connect more authentically. Trauma may have influenced your patterns, but awareness gives you the power to change them.

CHAPTER 5

# Trauma in the Workplace—an Expert's Perspective

*"The story doesn't end with trauma—it continues with how you choose to respond."*

***—Melissa Paty, MSN***

We've explored how the DISC framework can help us understand behavior styles in professional and personal life. But behavior never exists in a vacuum. For many people, especially leaders, the way we show up in meetings, decision-making, and relationships is deeply shaped by our past experiences with trauma.

To bring a clinical lens to this conversation, I sat down with Melissa Paty, MSN, a retired clinical nurse specialist, who spent decades supporting professionals in health-care settings. She has seen firsthand the ways trauma hides in plain sight, influencing behavior, relationships, and leadership. As she put it, *"Unresolved trauma doesn't just stay buried. It leaks out in ways people often don't even realize—at work, at home, everywhere."*

When I asked her what unaddressed trauma looks like in professional life, she explained that it often reveals itself at extremes.

> *"Sometimes you see withdrawal—a leader who avoids interaction, sits quietly in meetings, and doesn't build relationships. Other times, you see the opposite: perfectionism,*

> *hyper-organization, or even creating chaos. Trauma can amplify natural tendencies. A Dominant personality might become controlling and harsh. A Steady type might disappear into silence and avoidance. It shows up in who talks in meetings, who avoids conflict, who has to be right."*

The consequences are real. Trauma doesn't only influence behavior; it can also manifest in physical and emotional breakdowns. Melissa recalled a vivid example: *"I remember a nurse leader who had a full-blown panic attack while presenting to her team. Everyone assumed she was confident and strong, but her trauma had been building for years. That moment was a breaking point."*

For others, it comes in the form of anxiety, depression, or even physical illness. Although science still struggles to isolate trauma as the sole cause of chronic disease, Melissa stressed that the link between unresolved emotional pain and long-term health problems is undeniable.

So why do people stay silent if the costs are so high? Fear and shame, Melissa told me, are the two biggest barriers.

> *"People worry that if they open old wounds, they'll unravel everything they've worked so hard to build. They've created a successful identity, and they're terrified of losing it. Shame is another layer—many don't want to admit something happened at all. And for some, the deepest fear is that by facing their past, they'll somehow become like the people who hurt them. So they stay quiet, even when the cracks are obvious to everyone else."*

Melissa pointed out that this silence doesn't only cost the individual. It creates carryover effects in organizations. Leaders hiding from their own trauma may lash out, avoid hard conversations, or foster cultures of mistrust.

Employees sense when something is off, and turnover and burnout follow. *"If you don't deal with your own trauma, it will absolutely show up in your leadership. You might become the boss who bullies without realizing it or the leader who avoids conflict at all costs. Either way, you're not leading from a place of wholeness, and the organization pays the price."*

Healing, however, is always possible. The first step, Melissa said, is not therapy or strategy but safety. *"The very first thing people need is one safe person or space where they can finally tell the truth. Nothing changes until you feel safe enough to share your story."* From there, simple tools like journaling and mindfulness can provide early pathways to reflection.

For those ready for professional help, she pointed to therapies like cognitive behavioral therapy (CBT) and dialectical behavior therapy (DBT).

> *"CBT reframes your thinking patterns. DBT teaches very practical skills for coping with stress and regulating emotions. But the key is finding a therapist who really understands trauma. You need more than someone you like—you need someone who knows what they're doing."*

Melissa also emphasized that trauma-informed workplaces make a measurable difference, sharing, *"Organizations that understand trauma reduce turnover. They build loyalty. People don't leave jobs as much as they leave unsafe environments. If leaders create safety—if they acknowledge trauma exists and give people space to be human—they'll see retention, trust, and performance all improve."*

In other words, trauma-informed leadership is not only the compassionate, human approach. ... It's practical. It influences the bottom line as much as it shapes culture.

Perhaps the most hopeful message Melissa offered was about growth.

> *"Trauma doesn't just vanish, but it can be reframed. I've watched people take what nearly destroyed them and turn it into empathy and strength. Posttraumatic growth is real.*

> *The story doesn't end with trauma; it continues with how you choose to respond."*

Her words underline what this book has been building toward: Healing isn't only a personal journey; it's also a professional responsibility. Leaders who take courageous steps to confront their own stories don't only transform their own lives. They influence the lives of everyone they lead.

## Reflection: Trauma in Leadership and Workplaces

- ***Where do I notice tendencies in myself—silence, perfectionism, overcontrol, or chaos—that might be connected to unresolved experiences?***

____________________________________________

____________________________________________

____________________________________________

____________________________________________

- ***How have undue feelings of fear or shame kept me from addressing patterns that are affecting my leadership or relationships at work?***

____________________________________________

____________________________________________

____________________________________________

____________________________________________

- ***What would creating a safe space for myself look like, whether with a trusted friend, mentor, or professional?***

---

---

---

---

- ***If I began leading from a place of wholeness, how might it change the way my team, colleagues, or organization experience me?***

---

---

---

---

The business of dealing with your own healing doesn't have to look the same for everyone. It may unfold quietly in private or within the support of the community, as you'll see in the stories that follow.

INTRODUCTION TO THE STORIES

# Hiding in Plain Sight

When I began writing this book, I knew I didn't want to write about trauma. I wanted to write *with* it. That meant including voices beyond my own. I wasn't interested in distant case studies or statistics without soul. Instead, I wanted you to hear directly from real people, courageous individuals willing to share experiences many of us keep hidden. These stories are unimaginably painful, raw, and profoundly human. The storytellers shared their stories with me and wanted to share them with you in the hope that their story would connect with you in a way that would move you to action—an action that would set you on a journey of healing, permanent healing, the kind of healing that leads to peace and quieting of your soul.

Each of these participants bravely said yes to sharing their stories, hoping their openness might help someone else feel less alone or prompt someone suffering in silence to seek help for the first time. The sad truth is that I didn't have to look far to gather enough stories to fill an entire book. In fact, I collected far more than could fit here, making this, perhaps, volume one.

I conducted a personal interview with each participant. Our conversations unfolded in coffee shops, over Zoom calls, and in quiet spaces where they felt safe speaking openly. Some cried; some laughed; most did both. Yet, we all shared the same goal: If telling these stories helps even one person, we've accomplished our purpose. For some, I was the first person they'd trusted with their story beyond their closest confidante. Others, like

Brielle Cotterman and Reggie Ford, regularly share their experiences publicly. Two of our contributors have even delivered TED Talks. Their courage is extraordinary. Yet, every story shared here remains sacred, raw, and deeply personal.

As the interviewer, I believe wholeheartedly that these stories must be told. Some questions simply have no answer: Why do such horrific events happen to innocent people? What compels monstrous behavior from individuals who started life like us—innocent babies in their mothers' arms? These mysteries aren't solved within these pages. Indeed, we'd likely discover layers of trauma in the backgrounds of the perpetrators as well, perpetuating a cycle that sadly seems endless.

Yet, our focus remains firmly set on hope and the promise of healing. I hope that by illuminating these experiences, I help you open pathways for change. I hope that the silence and spiritual devastation caused by trauma do not have to define your life. I hope that you, too, discover a spark of light leading you toward real living and purposeful healing.

## Reporting and Disclosure: A Crucial Perspective

A striking pattern emerged throughout my interviews: Not a single sexual abuse survivor featured here reported their sexual abuse to authorities at the time it occurred. Many waited years—even decades—before speaking openly to anyone at all.

## As you read each story, I encourage you to thoughtfully consider the following:

- What factors might have prevented them from speaking up at the time of their abuse?

- How might early disclosures and reporting have influenced their healing journeys as well as their personal and professional outcomes?

Understanding these patterns of silence and delayed disclosure is essential. It helps us recognize the immense complexity and internal struggles survivors face. Most importantly, it underscores the critical need to create environments rooted in openness, compassion, and genuine support that empower survivors to speak their truths without fear or shame.

**Note:** Each person featured in this book was given the choice of sharing their identity or remaining anonymous. To protect their safety and privacy, the names of most (not all) participants have been changed. What remains unchanged is the raw, unfiltered truth of their stories and their remarkable generosity in sharing them.

CHAPTER 6

# Alene's Story: The Journey Out of Self

*"Healing means that I must step into my shoes and own my voice. It means that I can accept my flawed self, that I can still struggle at doing this perfectly, and that I now know it's just okay."*

***— Alene***

In this chapter, I invite you to meet Alene. Alene is a bold and action-oriented leader driven by urgency, independence, and results. You will hear her story directly in her own unfiltered voice. Afterward, we will pause together to unpack the hidden costs of overperformance, the lasting shadow of trauma, and the transformative power of turning inward. Throughout this book, we will follow a structure of story first, followed by reflection, to illuminate the complexities of trauma and healing.

Her story begins below, in her own words. Take your time with it. Let it settle. There's wisdom here. There's pain, yes ... but also power.

Interview Dossier

**Name:** Alene (*pseudonym used to protect privacy*)
**Age:** 60
**ACE Score:** 5 out of 10
**DISC Natural Style:** D

## Background Snapshot

**Education:** Some college (did not complete degree)
**Socioeconomic Background:** Grew up in an upper-middle-class household
**Current Role:** Senior executive in logistics
**Years in the Working World:** Over 35 years
**Career Highlight:** Led a full departmental turnaround, increasing inventory accuracy from 72% to 99.9%

## Trauma Timeline

**First Trauma:** Age 10
**Duration of Abuse:** Approximately 13 years, ending at age 23
**Primary Abuser:** Family member by marriage
**Other Trauma:** Additional instances of rape and physical abuse
**Substance Use:** Began drinking at age 13

**Medical Conditions:** Thyroid removal, cervical cancer, full hysterectomy, anorexia in her twenties and early thirties.

He was not unfamiliar. Soon, he would become a piece of a puzzle I would learn to navigate for the better part of my life. He would, in fact, begin to groom me (as I would eventually learn), and in this process, I would begin to lean into this space. There is still bewilderment about how he dance of the sickness would slowly become part of my cadence in how the art of hiding, hating, and anger would permeate all facets of my life: mentally, physically, emotionally, and spiritually. It took decades to call these feelings by the proper name.

At ten years old, the dance was slow: He would cuddle me and call to me from the high school window. Like a hungry soul for attention, I would move in and soak in his adoration of me. For most of those ten years, I felt invisible, alone, as if I were dropped into the wrong family. It was a family of much energy, emotions, and dynamics that would play out among those who would rise through the process of gaining the attention of our parents.

So, when he showed up and started to shower me with this attention, it now makes sense that I would soak it up, like flowers wishing for the rains to come. At the same time, he gained my trust, and he and my sister were starting their own journey. The sickness would play out for years, and in time, the knowledge would unfold—messy, destructive, a corrosive web of deceit, tarnished with guilt and shame.

At thirteen, a trip to spend the summer with my perpetrator and sister would change my world. I left my home as a child and came home tarnished, confused with a part of me awakened and dead all in the same breath. My first time getting drunk would happen on that trip, as was the first awareness that my body was his playground, my mind his battlefield.

I remember awakening from the night out with my sister and him. She had left for work, and we were alone. I came to from sleep, groggy and sick. I awoke to him sitting on the bed, staring down at me. The sheets were moved off my body. He leaned in and kissed me. His hand trailed my body, and I lay still. I was immobilized and scared. The words spilled from his lips, *"Don't ever say anything to anyone. They cannot know."* The language would change over time to *"You are a drunk. Who will believe you?" "You are sick."* Over the years, the perplexities of his advances and words would become confusing and scary.

Every family event was tinged. Every family gathering was a game of cat and mouse. Every relationship I would end out of fear of them finding out how "sick" and "broken" I was. Drinking became my favorite pastime, not out of pleasure but necessity. In desperation, I would give in. No fight. I heard the words of my mother, odd words, a joke from childhood: *"Better be good, or we will send you to the orphanage we got you from."*

I was not adopted. At five, I packed a brown bag, waited on the stairs for my dad's arrival home, and asked him to take me back. He looked broken at the sound of my words. So, it goes without saying I was primed for the picking.

At twenty-three, after ten years of what started as an occasional drink, my life was falling apart in every direction; destruction and complete annihilation of oneself had come to a point of breaking. I was diagnosed as a chronic alcoholic. To continue drinking would very soon lead to death. For the first time, I heard these words, and within me, for the first time ever, I wanted to live. I wanted to live—to breathe, to become, to unfold. These were not the words I used, but I think deep within me, there was a thirst for becoming whole—as whole as we humans can become.

The journey began slowly. The reality was that the abuse continued. I was trying to stay sober and working through the process of shedding the layers of hurt and of anger, mostly fear. I would go to my meetings, work with my sponsor, and help others. I had only shared a general perspective of the abuse with one other family member. Yet, the messaging back was confusing. I understand why better today. But for quite some time, I just put up with his advances, showing up to my place, pushing himself on me, demanding my attention, killing my hopes and dreams.

I was still full of self-loathing, not feeling like a whole woman, and completely unworthy of real love. I was messed up when it came to having a healthy perspective on sex, and it showed in almost all my relationships; everyone was my escape, and I hoped that I would find a soft space to land. Yet, the truth was, until I could get help for the damage done to me, I would never be able to be awake in this life. I had become an expert at leaving my body when others touched me. I became an amazing chameleon, able to change for others so I got their attention, even if for just a night. I was the mastermind behind most of the destruction in my relationships; I would pull them in, but once it got too real, I would run. Push. Blame.

How would I ever heal when I allowed harm to be done to me over and over? I was told early in my sobriety that you are an adult. Stand up for you. How? Who would believe me? What happens when I take my full life into my realm and face this deep, dark abyss? Who will I become? The questions were endless, and there seemed to be no perfect answer. Drinking was not the solution. This I knew. Religion was too close to the hurt from childhood and the sting that was sickly woven in many of the people I was around.

In 1999, months before I was to be married, my sister got her voice, and although her ways were harmful to me, in an odd sort of way, she kicked the door to my dungeon fully open. The morning after she told him she was done, she called me. In her manipulative way, she asked me if I could confirm what came to her in her dream. She asked me if he had hurt me. She asked in a voice that curdled my insides, the voice that always pulled me with sweetness and kicked me in the teeth with hate. Once I confirmed, within hours, she would begin to lay out the plot: She called priests and family members to tell them I had an ongoing affair with her husband. Calls began to pour in: "*How could you?*" was how most of the calls began. I was broken. I wanted to die.

Where was God?

In time, my story would become my story.

Did I contemplate suicide? Yes. Did I act as if my life was perfect? Absolutely. I went overboard with work, performing at peak performance, giving it my all. Equally, I tried to manage the household with precision, obsessively so to the point that I began to crack.

I couldn't keep it all together. Things with my family were tense and unpredictable. That looming feeling of being a fraud was ever present, that feeling of not being whole, a gnawing ache within my soul.

Was this what "healing" was supposed to feel like?

It is still amazing how teachers show up at the right time. I had met an amazing lady who would become my sponsor in AA (Alcoholics Anonymous). She told me the words that gave me permission to seek help. She said, *"I can help you with your thinking problem, but you need to seek outside help."* With her guidance and the support of my husband, who stayed by my side in a steadfast manner, I finally sought out help.

For two years, each week, I sat with a therapist who gave me a safe space to excavate the insides of my soul, allowing light to slowly slip into the spaces of darkness. In this process, I began to slowly unpack the shame, the guilt, the pain, the hurt, the haunting nightmares. I began to own my voice. It was but a beginning. The healing is ongoing. It never ends. I am not the abuse. I am not damaged. I am and will continue to heal. I still have a therapist today. At fifty-eight and almost thirty-five years sober, I am keenly aware that healing is not a one-and-done deal. It will be a part of my ongoing journey. My story, as I am learning, will be to help another begin their journey.

In the early stages of my recovery journey, I became deeply involved with AA. I actively participated in meetings, and when I felt ready, I eagerly took on the role of sponsor, mentoring and guiding other women who were navigating their own paths toward recovery. My ongoing dedication to AA has allowed me to support and inspire hundreds of women over the years. AA has become a cornerstone of my healing journey, providing me with a powerful sense of accountability, community, and personal growth.

Healing continues within the family. It is part of my marriage. It is part of my story. Healing will always begin with acknowledgment of an injury, a harm, violent words, or actions. Healing can begin with acknowledging the sense of dismissal, for this is how I learned the art of leaning into owning others' sickness and taking it on.

I am no longer the child who heeds the idle or real threats and cowers down. I am no longer able to feel whole when I remain in a place of perpetual manipulation, guilt, shame, or judgment. Healing means that I must step into my shoes and own my voice. It means that I can accept my flawed self, that I can still struggle at doing this perfectly, and that I now know it's just okay. Healing means that in this beautiful mess I call my life, I can build a safe space inside and no longer need to make this a requirement of anyone else in my life.

## What We Can Learn from Alene's Journey

Alene's story is stunning not only for its vulnerability but for how clearly it reveals the complex intersections of trauma, performance, and healing. But unfortunately, according to CDC data, it's not rare. At least one in four girls and one in twenty boys in the United States experience child sexual abuse. It's a case study in what I call "high-functioning hurt." From the outside, someone like Alene might look unstoppable: career driven, articulate, polished. But beneath that exterior lives a deeply fragmented self—someone who learned early that invisibility felt safer than authenticity.

**Trauma Doesn't Always Announce Itself Loudly:** Alene was never taught how to identify or express what was happening to her, especially in a family that prized image over intimacy. This is a common thread in stories of emotional neglect. The absence of overt abuse doesn't make the impact any less real. The absence of comfort *is* the trauma. When children are left alone to make sense of complex feelings, they often grow up to be adults who struggle to recognize their own needs.

**Grooming and Gaslighting Change the Internal Narrative:** The early sexual trauma Alene experienced didn't only violate her body; it rewrote the story she told herself about who she was. She was called "sick." She was told no one would believe her. That kind of manipulation plants a seed of self-doubt that can grow into a lifetime of shame. It's no surprise that she began self-medicating and dissociating to survive.

Many survivors do. In fact, adults with histories of childhood abuse are approximately seven times more likely to experience alcohol abuse issues.

**Performance Becomes a Mask for Pain:** Alene's driven, intense, goal-oriented personality mirrors the traits she used to build a successful life on the outside. But her perfectionism wasn't a strategy for success; it was a shield. Work gave her something she could control when everything else felt chaotic. Overachieving gave her a reason to be needed, liked, or praised—when what she needed was to be safe, seen, and loved.

**Healing Is Not Linear, But It's Always Possible:** Alene's recovery journey wasn't a single lightbulb moment. It was a series of small decisions—telling the truth, asking for help, sitting in therapy, staying sober even when it hurt. Her healing wasn't neat. It was messy and human. Yet she continued. She kept showing up, even when her voice trembled. That's the real work. That's what makes her story so powerful.

**You Don't Have to Be "Done" to Be Whole:** Alene is still healing. She still checks in with her therapist. She still notices old patterns and sometimes slips into them. But she also recognizes them now, and that self-awareness is a victory in itself. Healing isn't about erasing the past. It's about reclaiming the present. And she's doing that—every single day.

## Reflections for the Reader

Take a breath here. Let Alene's courage sink in. Then ask yourself gently:

- *Are there patterns in your professional or personal life that echo your early experiences?*

- *How has your inner voice been shaped by your childhood environment?*

- *What survival strategies might have served you once but are no longer helping you thrive?*

- ***When was the last time you offered yourself grace instead of criticism?***

---

---

---

---

If Alene's story resonates with you, I hope it gives you hope as well.

You don't have to have it all figured out to start healing. You don't have to be fearless. You *do* have to be honest with yourself first. And you *do* have the right to speak, to feel, and to move forward on your terms.

Let this chapter serve as a reflection of how deep pain can hide behind high performance, and what it looks like to come home to yourself.

Your next chapter is still unwritten. Let's keep going with our next story …

CHAPTER 7

# Caleb's Story: Quiet Courage and Purpose-Driven Healing

*"I believe in healing, but I also believe in the process. I don't need it to be perfect. I just need it to be real."*

***—Caleb***

When I first sat down with Caleb (not his real name), I had no idea what he was going to share. We were scheduled to talk about trauma and professional growth, like all the interviews in this book, but I didn't know the weight he'd been carrying. I don't think he did either, not fully. What unfolded was a quiet, vulnerable story of early sexual abuse by a female church leader, an experience he'd tucked away for decades, unsure how to label it, unsure how to process it, and unsure if it even "counted" as trauma.

This is what so many survivors wrestle with, especially when the trauma was a single incident, or when the abuser doesn't fit the mold we've been taught to expect. And when the survivor is a man? The silence can be deafening. But Caleb was brave enough to open the door and let someone in. In doing so, he offered a glimpse into what healing can look like when we lead with compassion, purpose, and integrity.

**Interview Dossier**

**Name:** Caleb (*pseudonym used to protect privacy*)
**Age:** 46
**ACE Score:** 2 out of 10
**DISC Natural Style:** IS

## Background Snapshot

**Education:** Bachelor of Science
**Socioeconomic Background:** Grew up in a middle-class household
**Current Role:** Nonprofit director
**Years in the Working World:** 26 years
**Career Highlight:** Led the launch of a youth-focused pilot program that became a personal healing catalyst and professional mission

## Trauma Timeline

**First Trauma**: Age 12
**Duration of Abuse:** One week, with multiple instances
**Primary Abuser:** Female church leader (non-family)
**Other Trauma:** Emotional distress and confusion surrounding the aftermath
**Substance Use:** None

**Medical Conditions:** Heart attack at age 42, Type II diabetes, diagnosed anxiety and depression

Like the other participants in this book, Caleb and I were scheduled to talk about how trauma impacts professional life. What I was not expecting was how quietly powerful the conversation would be—how gently he would unfold a story that he had carried in silence for decades.

Caleb is the kind of person who immediately makes you feel at ease—thoughtful, kind. He speaks with clarity but not force. He listens more than he talks. And the work he does, directing a nonprofit that helps create safer environments for youth, is clearly driven by deep care.

As he began to share, I saw that care came from somewhere deeply personal.

*"I was twelve,"* he told me, *"and I was on a church mission trip. That's when it happened."*

The story he shared was one I had not heard before, not because of the abuse itself but because of how it looked.

*"I was assigned to a mission outreach group led by a college-aged group leader,"* he said, *"which, at twelve, felt like a big deal, as most of my friends were assigned to groups led by older adult leaders. I felt like it was a sign that our youth pastor trusted me to be a contributor to a group with a college-aged group leader. I felt I was mature for my age. I liked being around older teens and young adults. I felt like I didn't quite fit with kids my age."*

His twenty-two-year-old female group leader took an interest in him. She made him feel seen, smart, and special.

*"She was funny. She was confident. She was a senior in college. I looked up to her,"* he said. *"She treated me like I was older. Like I mattered. And yet, I couldn't understand why she was giving me attention."*

At first, that attention felt like a gift.

*"It felt like a friendship. I didn't know what grooming was. I just knew I liked the way it felt to be chosen and feel special."*

But it changed quickly.

*"One night, she pulled me aside when we were walking in a secluded area of the camp we were staying at. She kissed me. Then other things, including oral sex, happened. It was confusing. I didn't feel safe or right, but I also didn't know how to say that."*

In a similar fashion, it occurred a few more times that week. Then the trip ended, and he went home.

*"I never told anyone. I didn't have the language for it. It stayed foggy in my mind for years."*

This is something I've heard from so many survivors, especially men, especially when the abuser is female. There's this added layer of cultural silence, of internal confusion.

The questions that surface sound like this:

Does this count? Did I do something wrong? Is it my fault?

Caleb didn't talk to a therapist. He didn't journal. He did what so many people do: He kept going. He got older. He moved into nonprofit work. He started a career that led to multiple leadership opportunities.

*"I just didn't think about it much,"* he said. *"Or if I thought about it, I still didn't have a framework for it. It stayed buried."*

Until one day, it didn't.

*"It started to come up when I was leading a work project on child safety policies. I was writing guidelines for leaders of youth-serving programs. And suddenly, I was thinking about that trip again and the young adult woman who abused me. And I realized—I know what happens when safeguards aren't in place. Because it happened to me."*

This moment of clarity didn't break him. It grounded him.

*"It made my work more personal, not in a heavy way, but in a meaningful way. I started sharing parts of my story when I trained others. Not the details. Just enough to say: 'This matters.'"*

He was clear about something else, too: The work helped him heal.

*"I don't know if my path is the healthiest way,"* he admitted, *"but creating safety for others has helped me feel safe myself. I started to comprehend what happened, not as something I caused but something I endured."*

He's still never done formal trauma therapy. But that doesn't mean he hasn't done the work.

*"Therapy isn't the only path,"* he said. *"For me, it's been pouring myself into my work. Mentorship. Service. And slowly, just little by little, sharing my truth."*

Caleb's DISC profile is a blend of Influential and Steady. These are the connectors, the empathizers, the people who build trust, listen before they speak, and prioritize the needs of others, sometimes more than their own.

When we talked about that, he nodded.

*"I've always been more comfortable caring for others than advocating for myself. But I'm learning. I'm learning to name what I need. I'm learning that boundaries aren't selfish, they're sacred."*

He also talked openly about how this trauma affected his body: a massive heart attack at age forty-two, type II diabetes, chronic stress that he'd normalized for too long.

*"I used to say I just had a stressful job. But now I realize—it's cumulative. It's not just the workload. It's everything I didn't say. Everything I carried in silence."*

His faith plays a role in how he's processed all of this. But it's not the traditional kind of church talk. It's nuanced, honest, and more about grace than guilt.

*"I believe in healing,"* he said, *"but I also believe in the process. I don't need it to be perfect. I just need it to be real."*

And real it is.

## What We Can Learn from Caleb's Journey

Caleb's story is a reminder that courage doesn't always roar. It can also sound like quiet honesty shared after years of silence. His experience reveals how trauma can take root in confusion, especially for men who've been taught not to name their pain. Yet his journey also shows how purpose and compassion can grow from that silence, turning personal loss into protection for others. There's much to learn from the way he chose healing not as a moment, but as a lifelong practice of meaning and service.

**One Moment Can Change Everything:** Caleb's abuse happened over the course of one week, and for years, he questioned whether it even "counted." But trauma doesn't have to be ongoing to be real. A single incident can shape the way we move through the world, especially when it happens during critical developmental years.

**Men Carry Invisible Trauma, Too:** So many male survivors go decades without naming what happened to them. Caleb's story shows how silence can take root and how powerful it can be to break it, even gently, even years later. In fact, CDC data show that nearly half (48.7 percent) of male sexual assault victims experience their first assault as adults. However, 51.3 percent first experienced assault as minors, with 26 percent experiencing victimization at age 10 or younger.

**Helping Others Can Be Part of Healing:** While it's not a substitute for therapy, purposeful work can be a powerful tool. Caleb found clarity, self-respect, and empowerment through the programs he managed to protect others. In helping create safety for others, he created it for himself.

**Compassion and Accountability Can Coexist:** Caleb doesn't excuse what happened. But he also acknowledges the complexity of it. "I have compassion for her," he said. "Something was broken in her, too." That kind of grace doesn't erase responsibility—it honors humanity.

**DISC Can Help Clarify How We Respond to Trauma:** Caleb's IS profile—empathetic, steady, peace-seeking—played a role in both his vulnerability and his healing. It helped him become a leader people trust but also meant he had to learn how to protect his energy and set firmer boundaries.

## Reflections for the Reader

As you reflect on Caleb's story, consider:

- ***Have you ever minimized your trauma because it "wasn't as bad" as someone else's?***

___

___

___

___

- ***Have you held silence around something that felt confusing or hard to name?***

___

___

___

___

- ***In what ways have you used work, service, or leadership as a path to healing?***

- ***Are you giving yourself the same compassion you offer to others?***

Caleb's story reminds us that healing doesn't always look like a breakthrough. Sometimes, it looks like showing up every day, doing the work, and taking small steps toward wholeness, even if no one else sees it.

There's no single path. But there is always a path. And you don't have to walk it alone.

CHAPTER 8

# Brielle's Story: Surviving the Unthinkable to Rewrite Her Future

*"Because I survived, I choose to speak."*

***—Brielle Cotterman***

Every time I meet with Brielle Cotterman, I'm immediately blown away by the poise and confidence with which she carries herself. In preparation for this book, we met virtually on a bright, early morning, and despite her busy schedule—including a prestigious speaking engagement at the Inc. 5000 conference—she made plenty of time to open up and share her experience with me. Unlike many of the interviews I've conducted, Brielle chose not to remain anonymous. She made it clear from the start that sharing her name publicly was intentional, a deliberate step toward reclaiming her story and empowering others.

Brielle's journey also stands apart from the others in this book because her trauma didn't begin in childhood—it occurred first in adulthood, layered with complexities of domestic violence and psychological manipulation. Her story underscores a different yet equally powerful truth: Trauma can strike at any age, and its impact can deeply alter how we see ourselves and navigate our professional lives.

## Interview Dossier

**Name:** Brielle Cotterman (*real name used with permission*)
**Age:** 42
**ACE Score:** Adult-onset trauma (intimate partner violence)
**DISC Natural Style:** Id

## Background Snapshot

**Education:** Bachelor of Science; completed all but two courses toward a Master of Business Administration

**Socioeconomic Background:**
Grew up in an affluent household

**Current Role:** Founder and CEO, Influential Leader Agency

**Years in the Working World:** 20+

**Career Highlight:** Transforming her public relations agency by quadrupling revenue and reshaping it into a purpose-driven business that empowers others to share impactful stories, directly inspired by her personal journey of overcoming domestic violence and discovering healing through storytelling.

## Trauma Timeline

**First Trauma:** Age 27 (escalating significantly around age 29–30)

**Duration of Abuse:** Approximately 3 years, culminating in her spouse attempting to murder her

**Primary Abuser:** Spouse (at the time)

**Other Trauma:** Emotional abuse, mental abuse, gaslighting, psychological manipulation, physical threats (grabbing, shoving, tackling), controlling behavior

**Substance Use:** None

## Health History

- Diagnosed with anxiety and PTSD
- Tumor on right adrenal gland, stress related
- Previously diagnosed autoimmune disease

When Brielle first spoke with me, she described her younger self as vibrant and driven. From the outside, her early adult life appeared picture-perfect. She shared:

*"I have always been a classic overachiever; good student, class president, on the homecoming court, beauty queen, and champion equestrian. However, as I was growing up, I collected a long line of limiting beliefs: people pleasing, perfectionism, equating love with accomplishments and praise, and always seeking to make everything 'fine,' or in other words, perfect."*

*"I never grew up with abuse,"* she shared candidly. *"I never expected to find myself in that situation. I was educated, successful, confident—or at least I thought I was."*

Brielle's relationship began as what she described as a *"whirlwind romance"* filled with intense love bombing, extravagant gestures, and promises of an idyllic future. Her partner was older, successful, charismatic—someone who initially made her feel special, valued, and admired.

*"I was swept away,"* she recalled. *"He had this incredible charm. I looked up to him because of his success, his intellect. It was intoxicating."*

After this whirlwind courtship, they were quickly married, and that charm gradually gave way to control. Small, seemingly innocuous behaviors—like comments about the color of her nail polish, the clothes she wore, or her choice of shoes—began to escalate. Slowly, the person she thought she knew became someone else entirely.

*"He'd get upset if my nails weren't the color he liked,"* she explained. *"It felt strange, but then he'd apologize and make it seem so reasonable. I'd think, 'It's just nail polish. If this makes him happy, why not?'"*

Over time, these isolated incidents transformed into a pattern of control and manipulation. *"He started controlling how I spent my time, who I saw, where I went,"* she said. *"I didn't see it happening at first. It was gradual and subtle."*

The controlling behaviors grew more severe, eventually including financial abuse. Brielle shared openly, *"He controlled all of our finances. Even though I had a successful career, I found myself financially dependent, asking permission for everything I spent."*

As the abuse intensified, Brielle described the psychological manipulation she endured: *"Gaslighting was a huge part of my experience. He convinced me that I couldn't trust my own memories or perceptions. Eventually, I questioned everything about myself."*

Brielle shared quietly. *"I knew then, deep down, how dangerous this had become."*

By the time Brielle realized what was happening, she was trapped, financially dependent, isolated from her support network, and disoriented by the psychological tactics her husband used to maintain control.

The abuse reached its devastating peak shortly after Brielle filed for divorce at age thirty. One afternoon, her husband appeared at their home unannounced, his intentions unmistakably violent.

*"He held the gun to my head and pulled the trigger...and it misfired."*

His words still echo in Brielle's memory. His chilling final threat was as clear as it was cruel:

*"If I can't have you, nobody's going to have you."*

Through sheer survival instinct, Brielle managed to escape his presence and barricade herself in another room, but he continued his relentless campaign to end her life.

*"I was able to lock the door behind me,"* she recalled. *"He fired nine rounds through that door. In his mind, I think he thought he had successfully killed me."*

Ultimately, she escaped through a window, at which point he turned the gun on himself, ending his own life.

This unimaginable incident left Brielle in profound fear and anxiety. *"I was barely living at that time,"* she confessed. *"I was terrified. I had to sit in the middle of the room away from the windows. I couldn't sleep through the night. There's no way to fully describe what it's like when a person you're supposed to trust tries to take your life."*

Through immense struggle and emotional pain, Brielle credits her survival largely to her faith. *"I know that if it weren't for my faith, I wouldn't be here,"* she emphasized quietly but deeply.

In the aftermath, Brielle grappled with intense shame, magnified by relentless media coverage that thrust her trauma into the public eye. Headlines were everywhere, portraying her in a misleading and damaging light. Brielle shared

*"People often say, 'Why didn't you just leave?'". They didn't understand the complexity or the danger involved."*

With no opportunity to respond or clarify the truth, Brielle found herself forced onto a stage she never wanted, stripped of control over her own story. She resolved then that she would never again let others dictate her narrative. Sharing her story became her way of reclaiming power, ensuring the truth was finally heard in her own voice.

In fact, the National Domestic Violence Helpline has collated data that shows people in abusive relationships take, on average, seven times to leave for good. Brielle's experience aligns closely with this reality, and once she finally broke free, her journey to reclaim herself was multifaceted and intensive.

Her path to healing involved extensive therapy, Eye Movement Desensitization and Reprocessing (EMDR) treatment, meditation, breathwork, and a fiercely dedicated commitment to physical health. *"Meditation saved me,"* she explained. *"It was the first time in years I felt I had control over my mind and body again."*

She also became deeply invested in advocacy, helping other survivors share their stories and heal. *"Speaking openly became my superpower,"* she said passionately. *"It not only helped others; it freed me."*

Professionally, the impact was profound. Brielle's experience reshaped her entire business approach. *"I realized I didn't want to help people become famous; I wanted to help people change the world."* Brielle reoriented her public relations firm, focusing exclusively on purpose-driven leaders committed to making a meaningful impact.

The decision to publicly share her story was transformative. *"When I finally found the courage to speak openly, my business quadrupled,"* she revealed. *"But it wasn't just about business growth; it was about reclaiming my story, my identity, my worth."*

Today, Brielle uses her voice and professional expertise to advocate fiercely for other survivors. As a TEDx speaker, renowned public relations expert, and founder and CEO of Influential Leader Agency, she leverages her personal story as a catalyst for deep, enduring impact and healing.

She has since shared her message on prestigious stages, including the Inc. 5000 conference, and has been recognized for her ability to merge advocacy with entrepreneurship. By helping leaders and professionals embrace vulnerability and share their authentic stories, she has created a "butterfly effect" that extends far beyond her own survival, transforming her clients' careers and changing cultural conversations about trauma and resilience.

Brielle openly acknowledges that owning her survivor narrative was once her greatest challenge due to the immense shame and fear surrounding her experience. *"I had a life that looked fabulous on the outside,"* Brielle shared, *"but my reality was far from shiny and perfect."*

It took a client's gentle encouragement, reminding her, *"If you don't share your story, you can never truly make the impact you are destined to make,"* for Brielle to courageously break free from her fear.

Since embracing her story, Brielle has transformed it into a powerful tool for social change and advocacy. She emphasizes the importance of recognizing subtle, nontraditional signs of domestic abuse, providing educational resources, and shifting cultural conversations about domestic violence to reduce stigma and shame. Her personal survival not only liberated her from self-imposed silence but also became the foundation for her professional mission: teaching others how to leverage their own experiences for meaningful change.

Through storytelling and media training, Brielle guides entrepreneurs and changemakers to authentically share their experiences, building stronger connections and greater societal impact.

Brielle's story is a powerful testament to her character, advocacy, and leadership. She reminds us that healing isn't about erasing our past but integrating it into a story we intentionally rewrite—one that fuels both personal peace and professional impact.

Her message is clear: Your story matters, and your voice has the power to transform not only your life but the lives of others.

# Warning Signs of Abuse

In addition to sharing her personal story, Brielle has worked to educate others on the subtle and not-so-subtle indicators of abuse. These warning signs continue to serve as a resource she shares in her advocacy and speaking work. She urges every reader to not only look for these signs in relationships, but also to reflect on why certain behaviors might ever be tolerated and to reevaluate one's relationship with self-worth and self-love.

Brielle emphasizes that these are not signs of a "rough patch" or a relationship that needs work. This is abuse. Naming these behaviors for what they are is the first step toward breaking cycles of silence and reclaiming power.

**Learn More About Brielle Cotterman's Work:** At Influential Leader Agency, Brielle Cotterman and her team connect visionary leaders with transformative opportunities. Their programs specialize in elite thought-leadership development, professional interview preparation and strategy, and media and speaking training designed to help experts share their stories with purpose and impact.

Learn more at www.influentialleaderagency.com.

## What We Can Learn from Brielle's Journey

**Trauma Can Happen to Anyone:** Brielle's story dismantles stereotypes often associated with domestic abuse. Abuse does not discriminate—crossing socioeconomic, educational, and demographic boundaries. The CDC reports that 41 percent of women in the United States experience sexual violence, physical violence, or stalking by an intimate partner during their lifetime. That means abuse touches every workplace, community, and professional circle.

**Early Red Flags Are Critical to Recognize:** Control and manipulation rarely begin as outright violence. They surface first in subtle, seemingly "harmless" behaviors that build over time. Recognizing these nontraditional red flags early can prevent escalation and even save lives. Domestic violence remains severely underreported, especially among higher socioeconomic groups, according to the CDC, where appearances of "success" may mask ongoing harm.

**The Strength of Public Vulnerability:** When Brielle chose to speak her truth publicly, she discovered that vulnerability is not weakness but power. Professionally, her willingness to be open not only expanded her influence but also created deeper trust with clients and colleagues, proving that authenticity fuels both healing and leadership.

**When Trauma and Professional Identity Intersect:** Brielle's healing journey reshaped her entire career. By integrating advocacy into her work, she discovered alignment between her personal story and her professional mission. Her experience highlights how addressing trauma can unlock clarity, authenticity, and purpose in leadership and business.

**Healing Is Holistic and Lifelong:** Brielle's recovery drew from multiple modalities—EMDR therapy, meditation, breathwork, faith, and physical fitness. Her example underscores that healing is not a single milestone but an ongoing discipline, one that strengthens and sustains professional performance over time.

## Reflections for the Reader

As you absorb Brielle's courageous journey, consider these questions:

- ***Have you ever questioned the validity of your trauma because it didn't look like what others expect?***

____________________

____________________

____________________

____________________

- ***Where might subtle patterns of control, manipulation, or gaslighting be present in your relationships, leadership, or workplace culture?***

________________________________________

________________________________________

________________________________________

________________________________________

- ***What possibilities might open if you shared more of your truth in safe spaces—whether privately or publicly?***

________________________________________

________________________________________

________________________________________

________________________________________

- ***What boundaries or practices can you establish to reclaim your power, voice, and sense of safety?***

________________________________________

________________________________________

________________________________________

________________________________________

Brielle's experience is a testament to endurance, advocacy, and leadership. By speaking her truth, she reclaimed what others once tried to control and redefined her life on her own terms. Healing, for her, has not meant erasing what happened but finding strength in what once threatened to break her. Her story reminds us that even the heaviest experiences can become a source of wisdom, guiding how we lead, connect, and choose to create change.

CHAPTER 9

# Michelle's Story: Breaking the Silence to Find Her Strength

*"I feel like the greatest gift that I have to give is giving back, helping others in their darkest moments to see the light."*

***—Michelle***

Michelle's voice, raw and clear, will walk you through her pain, struggles, and victories, creating space for empathy, recognition, and reflection.

Take your time reading Michelle's story. There's courage here, there's soul, and above all, there's hope.

## Interview Dossier

**Name:** Michelle (*pseudonym used to protect privacy*)
**Age:** 37
**ACE Score:** 7 out of 10
**DISC Natural Style:** DI

## Background Snapshot

**Education:** Master's degree

**Socioeconomic Background:** Middle-class upbringing

**Current Role:** Child abuse prevention coordinator

**Years in the Working World:** 20 years (since age 18)

**Career Highlight:** Achieved a significant promotion with a large salary increase; instrumental in providing training and resources to prevent child abuse within her community

## Trauma Timeline

**First Trauma:** Approximately age 5

**Duration of Abuse:** Approximately 4 years

**Primary Abuser:** Biological father

## Other Trauma:

Emotional and psychological manipulation; chronic fear

Extensive emotional abuse and severe body shaming

## Substance Use:

- Alcohol abuse initiated as a teenager; escalated during college
- Multiple Driving Under the Influence Incidents

## Health History

- Diagnosed with bipolar disorder
- Self-harm; history of severe depression, anxiety, and PTSD

Here's her story in her own words:

Looking back, I can't remember the first time any of it happened. Part of this lapse in memory can simply be blamed on the passage of time. But there is more at play here. For one, I didn't know that what was happening was wrong. In my head, it made sense that any part of their daughters' bodies should be available to be touched by their daddies. Bad daughters deserved beatings with belt buckles for their wrongdoings. And overweight daughters need to know they would have a better life if they weren't "*such a fat ass.*" Why would I remember the timing of events that, to me, were so normal?

It also cannot go without saying that, as time passes, many people find themselves blocking out traumatic events. Our minds and our bodies don't want to remember pain. My brain has found ways to prevent easy access to some of those most horrific moments of my childhood. But what I do remember is enough.

My father spent a lot of time watching television in his rocking chair while gnawing on his chewing tobacco. He would wear nothing but his tighty-whitey underwear even in my presence. It was not uncommon for my father to demand I sit in his lap like this. I remember the way he would shift my body to a position that was "comfortable" for him then abruptly stop and tell me to leave him alone. I had no idea what had happened for all those years.

When I was eight years old, my parents took me to Disney World. My memories of what should have been a joyous vacation are tainted by my father's disgusting and hurtful actions when he chose to abuse me once again sexually. My mom unknowingly saved me from further abuse by walking in and interrupting him. She still says that my father is the only person she knows who could ruin a trip to Disney World—little did she know.

My father was great at grooming me. He knew how to lure me into his trap and make me feel like he cared by buying me gifts and taking me to fun places. I remember him bringing me a pair of red and white cowgirl boots he knew I wanted, only to use my body later that night. He would also tell me he loved me at odd times. After hitting me, he would become calm and tell me how much I meant to him. Such contradictions confused my young mind, and I began to equate being spoiled with being hurt and being hurt with being loved.

I lived in fear. He promised that, if I told anyone, he would take me away and hurt me worse. His temper could lead to a physical attack at any moment. He could decide to touch me whenever he wanted. I became scared to sleep alone because the night left me vulnerable. I begged to sleep with my mom every evening, putting my faith in her ability to keep me safe.

I used food as comfort for much of my childhood, which gave my father another reason to throw attacks my way. I was not a small child, and he had no qualms calling me fat in front of people I knew. A friend recently shared that my father had once told her he wished he had a daughter her size instead of one he couldn't pick up.

It was a vicious cycle: He would taunt me about my weight, assault me. I would then eat to soothe the pain, and he would continue to ridicule my by-then mildly obese body.

At a very early age, I found myself desperately seeking my father's approval. I became obsessed with maintaining all As on my report cards, tried my best to have perfect behavior, and aimed to excel at playing the piano. In my mind, being perfect was my best shot at protecting myself. If I could prove I was worthy, maybe he would love me. As it turned out, I would never be enough.

*"I don't want to go home. Daddy will hurt me again."*

It was a Saturday afternoon in October. I was nine years old. My mom and I were visiting my grandparents at their neighborhood yard sale. My mom's brother and sister-in-law, and my uncle and aunt, were there, too. It had been a long, busy day, and most kids would have been ready to go home to their toys and air-conditioning. When my mom announced it was time for us to leave, however, I stopped breathing for a moment.

I didn't want to go home. He was there.

My mom began gathering our things and loading her red Bronco. With her gone, I ran into my grandmother's arms. According to my aunt, it was as though a dam broke inside me.

*"Please don't make me go,"* I choked through my tears. *"I can't go."*

Finally, I was able to tell them what was happening.

With the support and guidance of my grandparents, my mom quickly filed for divorce, and my father was out of the house. But that did not mean he was gone. On several occasions, he would drive by our home while I was playing outside, making threats and inappropriate comments. Additionally, the court ruled that I had to see my father at a counselor's office once a month. This hour-long meeting was torturous; I would cry with dread for days leading up to each session.

For a year and a half, I relived the trauma from my past just by seeing his face. The fear had not subsided just because we no longer shared a house.

As I hit pre-teen age, I also developed a fear of hugging any male family members. Physical contact with anyone, including my beloved grandfather, made me incredibly uncomfortable. In my mind, all men were like my father. To this day, I ask for female doctors, dentists, therapists, and other professionals when making appointments.

I became very depressed after the divorce, but I quickly found ways to *"cope."* At thirteen years old, I cut my wrists for the first time. On one hand, it was the self-inflicted punishment I felt I deserved. I didn't like who I was, and I felt I should physically feel the pain. There was also something about it that made me feel alive when so much about my life seemed dead. Plus, the scars served as reminders of the pain that had plagued my life up to that point. As much as I wanted to forget, I also wanted to remember.

My family didn't understand why I'd resorted to hurting myself. *"Is this just a cry for help?"* they'd ask. Others accused me of doing it *"for attention."* I was sent to a therapist and put on medication. I felt judged, but not enough to stop, even after three trips to the E.R. for emergency stitches on my legs and arms.

When I was around age sixteen, promiscuity became the addiction of choice. While I continued to overeat and cover my body with cuts, I saw sex and male attention as the approval I'd always wanted. Being with older married men was particularly attractive. They were *"safe."* Because they were married, there were limits to how close they would get to me. To me, getting close meant getting hurt.

In my junior year of high school, I became involved with one of my teachers. In my teenage mind, the fact that this man was jeopardizing his family and his job must have meant I was worth something. Similar situations followed. I had sex with bosses, a college academic advisor, and fathers of kids I babysat. I cheated on my boyfriends to *"test"* how much of my selfishness they would tolerate before dumping me. I did not know how to have healthy relationships. All I knew about "love" was what my father had shown me.

I was eighteen when I had my first real experience with alcohol. My father had a drinking problem, and the half-brother I barely knew was also an alcoholic. Despite this, I somehow managed to avoid my drinking addiction until the summer after my senior year of high school. I was at a pool party when a friend handed me a can of Bud Light. It took only a few sips to realize how much I enjoyed the beer's taste and effect. Alcohol became my foremost "coping mechanism."

The next few summers, friends and I snuck our way into kegger parties on the nearby college campus. Before we ever got there, we would "pre-game" at home with whatever liquor I had been (unsuccessfully) hiding from my mom. Once we made it to whatever party we found, we would drink copious amounts of cheap beer from red Solo cups. I would drive home totally obliterated, only to awaken without remembering how the night ended.

I started college in 2005. The East Coast made for a completely different campus experience. During the school year, clubs and bars replaced the kegger parties I was used to back home in the South. Fake IDs were easy to come by, and men were eager to buy drinks for college students they hoped they could seduce. Every weekend was an opportunity to drink myself to the point of blacking out. I even filled water bottles with vodka to take to class. Despite this, I maintained my grades and managed to avoid any major consequences for my quickly developing alcoholism.

In the spring of my freshman year, I was struck by another traumatic experience. While drinking at a party, I was drugged and raped by a complete stranger. A couple of men my friends had met at a bar invited us to attend their luau-themed party in the financial district of NYC. According to my friends, they turned around on the dance floor, and I had disappeared. At some point in the night, someone drugged my drink and managed to sneak me to their apartment.

There is a huge gap in what I remember from that night. I do recall waking up for a brief minute and seeing a stranger on top of me, both of our clothes off, my body completely paralyzed. I blacked out again after that. When I became conscious the second time, I found that the man was in the bathroom. I pulled on my clothes as quickly as I could and ran out the door. Still groggy, I made it home to my apartment, where I isolated myself with endless liquor. To this day, I do not know who my rapist was or where it all happened.

For the next two weeks, I did not leave my apartment except to replenish my supply of alcohol. I didn't attend classes, and I avoided all my friends. I felt dirty, hurt, and even mad at myself for letting something like this happen. For months, my stomach stayed in knots, and I'd get sick frequently. As it turns out, these symptoms weren't caused by an emotional response to the rape.

I was pregnant, and I knew it was his.

I found out about the pregnancy one week after school ended in May 2006. I was at my yearly gynecologist appointment, and, per routine, the nurse had me urinate in a cup. A few minutes later, she took me into a room and told me the news. I broke.

I had finally opened up to my mom about the rape a few months earlier. When I told her I was pregnant, she immediately knew who the father was and began to cry. Knowing I needed her completely, she encouraged me to make the choice I felt I needed to make for myself. I had no doubt she would support me, whatever decision I made. In tears, I told her I needed to have an abortion, and she held me, ensuring she was always on my side.

The next day, my mom drove me to Planned Parenthood. Protesters heckled us in the parking lot, screaming that I was a "*baby killer*" and that God didn't love murderers. My mother firmly replied, "*Until your daughter gets pregnant by a rapist, you don't get to say a word to her.*" I treasured her unconditional support, but I still felt a surge of guilt as I walked through those doors.

A handful of women were waiting inside the lobby. Each of us went through the same process: basic paperwork, a consultation with a nurse, the procedure itself, and time in the recovery room. My state's law requires all women to be shown an ultrasound, and while this step chilled me completely, I knew that I could not have this child. I was too young, too immature, and too unprepared to experience the birth of my rapist's baby.

The actual procedure was physically unbearable. While my mind was whirling and my emotions spun out of control, my body experienced a pain I had never felt without any anesthesia. I felt everything. The intense cramping continued to haunt me for days.

Despite concerns about my capacity to function after the abortion, I returned to the East to finish my undergraduate degree the next semester. After graduation, I had the opportunity to study and teach across Europe. Although I got to travel to multiple countries during this time, many memories were left unmade thanks to the amount of time I spent drunk or hungover.

Regrets still abound.

My drinking continued to worsen after I graduated from college. I lost a job due to poor performance during a hangover. I lost my fiancé because of the numerous fights (and mutual cheating) that occurred after heavy drinking. My alcoholism had exploded into a full-fledged crisis, and as I started graduate school in 2010, the legal ramifications began to pour in.

I received my first DUI in the 2010s. I had only recently moved to a new city and didn't have many friends. I decided to go to a nearby bar to meet people and, more importantly, engage in heavy drinking. I befriended the drummer of the band that was playing at the bar and made plans to continue our conversation with a nightcap at my apartment. While waiting for him outside while he packed up his equipment, a police officer approached my car for a *"courtesy check,"* as mine was the only vehicle left in the front lot. While talking to me, the officer smelled alcohol on my breath and had me complete a field sobriety test. Unsurprisingly, I failed.

I had never started my car and was sitting with the engine off, so I assumed I was safe from a DUI. However, I soon learned that having keys in the ignition is enough to warrant the charge. I was still *"in control of the vehicle."* My charges were reduced to reckless driving, but I was required to serve forty-eight hours in the county jail. Although I slept through the majority of my sentence, I saw enough to know I never wanted to experience jail life again. Unfortunately, that first offense wasn't enough to keep me from drinking and driving.

The next spring, I was pulled over a second time. I had once again been drinking at a bar. According to the officer, the original purpose of the stop was to inform me of expired car tags. Once again, the smell of alcohol on my breath was obvious, and I failed another sobriety test. Because the first charge had been reduced, this second arrest ended up being a first-offense DUI, which also warranted another forty-eight-hour sentencing. I also received a violation of probation charge since there had only been eight months between the first and second offenses. Because I had been in the city limits, I spent my time in a different jail, but the experience was much the same. I mostly kept to myself and remained in my cell, sleeping or reading one of the few books they had available. When the forty-eight hours were up, I once again swore I would never return.

Then the second offense (third arrest) DUI came in 2011. I had been attending a tacky Christmas sweater party and was decked out for the celebration. I had been so drunk that most of the party escapes my memory now. I also don't remember being pulled over, but, according to the officer, I had been driving on the wrong side of the road. That night, I spent four hours in a cold holding cell wearing sequins, bells, and boas and feeling like an absolute idiot. A few months later, I would spend forty-five days in jail.

My six weeks in jail were a lot different than my two-day experiences there. It didn't take long to realize that I would not be able to sleep through my forty-five-day sentence. After a few days, I made my way to the open pod area and began talking with some of the other ladies. Many of them were working on obtaining their GEDs and requested my help. Both bored with card games and interested in these women's futures, I spent the remainder of my sentence tutoring them in math and language skills. Although I hated my time there, it was nice to feel like I had a purpose.

Throughout the year and a half of arrests and jail time, I made a few half-hearted attempts at "*fixing*" my drinking problem. I still did not see myself as a true alcoholic and argued that I could stop anytime. Despite these delusions, I agreed to attend an intensive outpatient program and a partial hospitalization program. These short-term group sessions offered twelve-step program advice, which I understood cognitively but could not seem to put into practice.

After the second DUI conviction, I agreed to attend a forty-five-day inpatient rehab program. I participated in group and individual therapy, daily twelve-step meetings, and a slew of activities to expand my ability to cope in healthy ways. I loved rehab. I met great women who shared similar experiences, pains, and addictions. I learned to use art, yoga, and animal companionship (through equine therapy) to relieve the trauma of my past and the stresses of my present. And I slowly began to recognize how my alcoholism was destroying my life and the lives of those around me.

I stayed sober for nearly five months before I picked up my first post-rehab drink. No single event prompted the decision to return to alcohol; I merely liked and missed its effect. At this point, I was drinking a box of wine or a pint of liquor—whatever it took to black out—each night. I was still acting out sexually, desperately seeking approval from men. And my emotional state had plummeted again; I hated who I was. My depression had reached a new high, and booze helped me escape the emotions I did not want to feel.

By the mid-2010s, I felt like I couldn't take it anymore. After a few margaritas and several shots of whiskey with friends, I got in my car and texted my mom, "*I'm so sorry.*" I had decided I was tired of living.

That afternoon, I sped my car into a brick wall.

Reports stated that my engine was on fire when responders made it to the scene. The entire front half of my vehicle had been flattened by the impact, crushing me between my seat and the steering wheel. I was later told no one expected me to live.

The only memory I have of that night is waking up in an ambulance and saying, *"I couldn't even kill myself right."*

When I regained consciousness the next day, I saw a ticket for a DUI lying on the table beside my bed. I was terrified of the minimum jail sentence and the resulting consequences. However, because my wreck was a suicide attempt, my case was moved to mental health court. I did not have any jail time but was required to attend bimonthly therapy sessions and was tested for drugs and alcohol at least once a week. The judge did not treat me like a criminal but as a human who needed special help. I remained sober for over a year, but only out of fear of the legal consequences of a relapse.

Stupidly and selfishly, I went through one more month-long drinking spell. I returned to my nightly blackouts despite friends' discouragement and my own personal guilt. By the time I was ready to call it quits, months had been spent in jail, psychiatric, and rehab facilities. My mother had spent tens of thousands of dollars on bail, attorney fees, and rehab programs. I had ruined relationships, faced sexual assaults, and had elevated my self-hatred to a suicidal level.

It took my grandfather's death for me to make the final promise. In 2017, my grandpa got very sick and was placed in hospice care. I spent the last few days of his life by his side, sharing memories and last-minute thoughts I'd refrained from ever saying. In his last hours, I held his hand and apologized for hurting him and our family for over a decade. I swore to him I would never touch alcohol again.

I have remained sober since 2017. Two years later, in 2019, my father died.

I wasn't invited to the funeral, and my name was left out of the obituary because my family didn't want to acknowledge what he had done. I was never informed whether I was granted anything in his will. In essence, even in his death, it was as if I never existed to him or that side of my family. They failed me from beginning to end. Over the years, I have been blessed with opportunities to use my life experiences to serve others. In my community, I worked at a home for women in recovery from addiction. The ladies who stayed there, all survivors of abuse, bravely shared their stories of trauma, addiction, and healing. I was honored to work alongside women overcoming their own trauma and addiction, women in whose shoes I have walked. I took great pride in showing them that surviving the trauma and subsequent addiction is absolutely possible—one day at a time!

These women were inspirational; their strength reaffirmed that I, too, am capable of rising above my demons. I also had coworkers and volunteer friends who welcomed me into their own families, providing safe spaces when I felt down or alone. I was constantly reminded of how lucky I've been to receive so much love and support throughout my chaotic life.

After moving back home, I took a rewarding position in child abuse prevention. Working with children who have been abused is now a calling. As a survivor, I know firsthand how much childhood trauma can damage a person long-term. I have seen the effects of addiction, crime, and emotional turmoil that can come as a result of abuse. As a result, I recognize that education and awareness are critical, and I feel honored to have joined the sexual abuse prevention community in taking the crucial first steps to eliminate child abuse.

I feel like the greatest gift that I have to give is giving back, helping others in their darkest moments to see the light, helping educate the community on issues surrounding sexual abuse and the ways we are working to prevent this scourge from our society.

A few years ago, driving home from work, I saw blue lights in my rearview mirror. Although I knew I had done nothing wrong, the mere sight of a police officer pulling me over made my stomach churn. The officer explained that he had stopped me as a courtesy to let me know my taillight was out. Following protocol, he ran my license and registration, and when he returned to my car, his face was white. *"I thought that was you,"* he said. Thinking this must have been one of the officers who had picked me up in one of my drunken stupors, I nervously laughed.

"No," he said. *"That night, at the wall. I was the first one there. I was the one who pulled you out of your car."* We both teared up. *"I always prayed for you and hoped you were doing okay. It's so good to see you here."*

I'm finally at the point where I'm glad I'm still here, too.

## What We Can Learn from Michelle's Journey

Michelle's story brings forward important themes that deserve our careful attention and understanding. Here's how her deeply personal story connects to broader lessons and insights:

**Trauma Deeply Influences Authority Relationships:** Trauma, particularly when experienced at the hands of a trusted authority figure like a parent, reshapes how we relate to power and authority throughout our lives. Michelle's fear and avoidance of male authority figures—doctors, therapists, even family members—highlighted a deep-seated mistrust born of early betrayal.

In professional settings, this can subtly translate into challenges in accepting guidance, hesitancy in building mentor relationships, and persistent anxiety around feedback.

**Subtle Self-Sabotage as an Unconscious Defense:** Michelle's repeated patterns of alcohol abuse, self-harm, promiscuity, and risky decisions were not isolated events but part of an unconscious, recurring cycle rooted in unresolved trauma. While outwardly successful, these self-destructive behaviors frequently sabotaged her progress, professional stability, and emotional health. Recognizing the source of these behaviors, unhealed trauma, was a crucial step toward breaking this cycle.

**The Complex Cost of Overachievement:** Michelle's relentless drive for academic and professional excellence reveals a common pattern among trauma survivors: using achievement as a shield against pain, rejection, and internalized inadequacy. Her need to perform perfectly, achieve highly, and appear flawless was less about ambition and more about a deep need to prove worth and earn approval, especially from authority figures. This pressure was exhausting and unsustainable but hard to relinquish.

**Breaking Silence as a Powerful Turning Point:** When Michelle bravely spoke up as a pre-teen, her disclosure was met immediately with belief and action, dramatically changing her trajectory. This supportive response underscores the power of validation and swift intervention in trauma recovery. When survivors courageously speak their truth and are met instead with denial, rejection, or blame, it can inflict secondary trauma, deepening their wounds and complicating their path toward healing.

Later, her willingness to openly share her story again as an adult became central to her own healing as well as her advocacy and empowerment of others; that courage to break the silence can be transformative at any age. Research indicates that children who receive affirming responses upon disclosing abuse tend to experience fewer trauma symptoms and shorter durations of abuse compared to those who do not receive such support.

**Healing is Ongoing, Messy, and Deeply Personal:** Childhood sexual abuse has been identified as a risk factor for alcohol problems in adolescence and adulthood. Research indicates that both child physical and sexual abuse are associated with alcohol abuse in adult women even when taking into consideration generational alcoholism.

Michelle's story underscores a recurring, important truth: Healing isn't linear, neat, or straightforward. Her journey involved setbacks, progress, relapse, and steady growth. True healing, she discovered, involves embracing support, developing healthier coping skills, and learning to trust oneself again. It's a lifelong commitment to self-awareness, patience, and grace. Through therapy, community service, medication management, journaling, and ultimately professional advocacy, Michelle found constructive ways to cope, stabilize, and rebuild her sense of self. She learned to acknowledge her pain openly without allowing it to define her entirely.

Michelle also reminds us that healing does not require perfection—it demands authenticity. It means recognizing when past patterns resurface and choosing to address them with compassion rather than criticism. It means allowing yourself to accept help, trust those who earn it, and prioritize your own emotional health above the performance or achievements that previously defined your worth. Michelle's courage to continue showing up, despite setbacks, highlights a crucial message for every survivor: You are never beyond healing, and every small step forward is meaningful.

## Reflections for the Reader

Take a quiet moment now, and let Michelle's story resonate. Reflect honestly on your own experiences, gently considering these questions:

- ***Are there ways you've noticed your past trauma shaping your interactions with authority, trust, or professional relationships?***

- ***Can you identify subtle patterns of self-sabotage or coping behaviors in your own life? If so, how might recognizing these patterns help you move forward differently?***

- ***In what ways have you leaned on success or productivity as armor against deeper pain?***

- ***Who in your life might you safely share your story with to begin releasing what you've carried alone?***

- ***What small step could you take to voice more of your truth in a safe place?***

---

---

---

---

Michelle's story illustrates that success on the outside doesn't always reflect peace on the inside. Healing begins when we name what we've carried, set down the burdens that no longer serve us, and step into a future defined by honesty, freedom, and strength.

# CHAPTER 10

# Savannah's Story: Navigating Shadows to Find Her Light

*"My story is messy, but it's mine. Healing is not about perfection; it's about embracing authenticity and trusting your own voice. We don't have to erase our past—we integrate it. We reclaim it and move forward with courage."*

***—Savannah***

When I met with Savannah, I immediately noticed her gentle strength and genuine warmth. As we began our conversation, it quickly became clear that her poised presence was not achieved easily; rather, it was hard-won through years of navigating shadows from her past.

Savannah's life has been profoundly affected by trauma. Yet, far from diminishing her, these experiences have given her remarkable insight and depth. She generously opened up about her journey, offering a candid glimpse into how hidden wounds can influence our professional paths, shape our relationships, and affect our very sense of self.

In this chapter, you'll hear Savannah's story directly from her. Together, we'll explore the complexity of unresolved trauma and, more importantly, the transformative power of reclaiming one's voice.

Take your time with her words. Within her story, you'll find wisdom born of pain but also the incredible strength and hope that come with doing the work to achieve healing.

## Interview Dossier

**Name:** Savannah (pseudonym used to protect privacy)
**Age:** 44
**ACE Score:** 9 out of 10
**DISC Natural Style:** CS

## Background Snapshot

**Education:** Bachelor's degree
**Socioeconomic Background:** Grew up in a middle-class household
**Current Role:** Successful entrepreneur and business owner
**Years in the Working World:** Over 25 years
**Career Highlight:** Founded and operates a successful business, providing leadership and mentorship in her community

## Trauma Timeline

**First Trauma:** Age 5, emotional and psychological abuse stemming from her mother's alcoholism
**Duration of Abuse:** Persistent emotional abuse and neglect throughout childhood
**Primary Abuser(s):** Mother and grandmother
**Other Trauma:** Sexual abuse at age 7 by a babysitter and babysitter's boyfriend; significant emotional abuse from maternal grandmother; later experienced emotional and verbal abuse in her marriage

**Substance Use:** None

## Medical Conditions:

- Ocular histoplasmosis syndrome (diagnosed in adulthood)
- Ehlers-Danlos Syndrome, a chronic condition characterized by joint instability and chronic pain
- Ongoing struggles with weight and health linked to unresolved trauma

In her mid-forties, Savannah is a bright and successful real estate entrepreneur, a dedicated mother of two, and a woman who knows a thing or two about reclaiming personal power. But her calm confidence today masks a troubling past that was hidden in silence for decades.

As our conversation unfolded, Savannah generously offered me a clear, unfiltered window into her life and how trauma has influenced it at every stage …

From her earliest memories, Savannah navigated emotional chaos within her family. Growing up with a mother struggling deeply with alcoholism, her childhood was defined by uncertainty and instability.

*"My mom was an alcoholic. I remember coming home from school and never knowing what I'd find,"* Savannah shared. *"Sometimes it was peaceful, sometimes chaotic. It felt like walking on eggshells every day."*

At age seven, Savannah experienced sexual abuse at the hands of her babysitter and the babysitter's boyfriend—an experience she never reported.

*"I didn't even understand what was happening,"* she told me. *"I just knew something felt very wrong. I had no words, no language. It stayed hidden."*

Her silence wasn't only a result of confusion; it was a protective response to the shame and uncertainty she felt. Like many survivors, Savannah internalized this trauma, carrying a heavy emotional burden into adulthood.

Further emotional trauma stemmed from Savannah's maternal grandmother, who consistently subjected her to intense verbal and emotional cruelty.

*"My grandmother was emotionally abusive,"* Savannah explained, visibly pained by the memory." *She would constantly tell me how worthless I was, that I'd never amount to anything. After hearing that so many times, I started to believe it."*

Savannah's self-esteem eroded steadily under this persistent emotional assault. Food became both her comfort and torment, leading to lifelong struggles with body image and self-worth.

*"Food was something I turned to for comfort. But then I felt even more shame when my family constantly commented about my weight,"* she revealed. *"It was a vicious cycle that started in childhood and continued well into adulthood."*

Additional instability came from her mother's multiple extramarital affairs and eventual arrest for drunk driving, reinforcing Savannah's fear and anxiety.

As an adult, Savannah's trauma continued, particularly through her marriage. Married at age twenty-two, Savannah faced ongoing emotional, verbal, and financial abuse from her husband.

Like so many women I spoke with in writing this book, her marriage mirrored earlier patterns of neglect and emotional cruelty.

*"My husband would criticize and control everything from finances to my self-esteem,"* Savannah confided. *"I stayed far longer than I should have, thinking this was what I deserved."*

After nearly two decades, Savannah found the strength and clarity to leave. The decision was terrifying but liberating.

*"Leaving my marriage was one of the hardest things I've ever done, but it was the first real step toward reclaiming myself,"* she affirmed.

In her mid-thirties, Savannah reached a turning point. She sought therapy, initially intending marriage counseling, but soon discovered the need to address her own unresolved trauma. Therapy became pivotal in her healing journey.

*"Therapy saved my life,"* Savannah shared openly. *"It was the first time someone helped me understand that my experiences were not my fault. Therapy taught me to see my trauma differently and to find my voice."*

Savannah also described the deeply painful loss of her sister, who died suddenly in a car accident at the age of twenty-three. This tragedy deepened her isolation and grief but also reinforced her determination to heal.

*"Losing my sister crushed me. But it also became this profound reminder to live fully, to heal and live the life she didn't get to live."*

At age forty, Savannah began a transformative new chapter by launching her real estate business. Becoming an entrepreneur was more than a professional move; it was an empowering act of self-discovery and independence.

*"Starting my own business felt like stepping into my truth,"* Savannah reflected with clarity. *"It was terrifying at first, but it became the place where I learned to trust myself and redefine success on my terms."*

Entrepreneurship provided Savannah with an avenue to confront long-standing insecurities. She discovered genuine confidence by overcoming internal doubts and external judgments, gradually recognizing that her value came from within.

Despite significant health challenges, including ocular histoplasmosis syndrome resulting in blindness in one eye, and Ehlers-Danlos

Syndrome—a chronic condition causing ongoing pain—Savannah remains steadfastly committed to healing and thriving.

*"These health conditions remind me every day of what I've been through, but they've also shown me the depth of my resilience. They challenge me, but they don't define me."*

Today, Savannah emphasizes the importance of intentional self-care and emotional management. She utilizes journaling, gratitude exercises, and spending mindful time outdoors to ground herself. Medication management and ongoing therapy remain central to her daily wellness.

Savannah defined healing clearly:

*"To me, healing means being able to fully enjoy life's moments without constantly fearing the worst," Savannah explained. "It means quieting that internal voice that always says, 'What if?' and learning to live in the now."*

Yet, Savannah admits that the process isn't always easy. Doubts still surface; challenges still emerge. But what sets her apart is the determination that refuses to let trauma dictate her future. She shared:

*"Every time I get to the point where I think maybe I'm not cut out for this, maybe this is not the place for me, there's a part of me that says, I'm not going to let this win."*

As our conversation concluded, Savannah's reflection revealed the core of her strength born not from the absence of fear but from her willingness to keep moving forward despite it.

*"My story is messy, but it's mine. Healing is not about perfection; it's about embracing authenticity and trusting your own voice. We don't have to erase our past—we integrate it. We reclaim it and move forward with courage."*

Today, Savannah mentors others, using her experiences as a source of strength and empathy. She has found purpose and meaning by openly sharing her story and actively guiding others on their paths to healing.

Entrepreneurship has not only allowed her professional success, but it has also given her the platform to encourage countless others, teaching them how trauma can be transformed into advocacy and leadership.

Savannah's unwavering commitment to healing serves as a powerful reminder that our past does not define us. It's never too late for our history to be reclaimed and ultimately used as a source of wisdom and strength.

## What We Can Learn from Savannah's Journey

Savannah's story reminds us that trauma doesn't just leave emotional scars. It reshapes how we trust, connect, and create meaning. Her journey traces the long arc between silence and self-definition, showing that reclaiming one's voice is both an act of courage and an act of reconstruction. Her strength lies in how she transformed suffering into self-awareness and leadership, modeling how reflective growth can replace reactive survival.

**When Authority Abuses Trust:** Savannah's early trauma made her wary of those in positions of guidance, including doctors, therapists, and mentors. For survivors, betrayal at the hands of authority figures often creates an unconscious belief that power and guidance come with danger or disappointment. As Savannah's story illustrates, this mistrust does not simply dissipate with age; it can infiltrate professional relationships, hinder leadership development, and restrict access to mentorship opportunities. Healing requires intentionally rebuilding trust through safe, affirming experiences over time.

**The Cost of Hidden Coping Patterns:** Savannah named how emotional eating and body-image struggles had roots in unresolved trauma. Although these behaviors once offered comfort and a sense of control, they later became self-sabotaging. Coping strategies like perfectionism, overcontrol, or avoidance often begin as a form of protection but, if left unexamined, can stand in the way of deeper healing. By confronting and naming these behaviors, Savannah created space for healthier practices, such as therapy, mindfulness, and daily self-care.

**The Courage of Speaking Truth:** Choosing to share her story became a turning point for Savannah. Speaking openly restored her voice and agency. Yet, her experience also highlights the risks: When survivors are met with disbelief or dismissal, they can experience secondary trauma. Her journey underscores the importance of safe, supportive environments where truth can be honored.

**Healing as a Lifelong Practice:** Savannah's story demonstrates that healing rarely progresses in a linear manner. Therapy, medication, journaling, mindfulness, and daily practices have all been part of her process. There have been setbacks, but progress comes through authenticity, self-awareness, and kindness toward herself. Healing is not about perfection but about persistence, growth, and integration.

**Entrepreneurship as Empowerment:** Founding her own business gave Savannah something she had never fully known before: control, autonomy, and confidence. Entrepreneurship became both a tool for personal recovery and a channel for advocacy; she now mentors other women in her community. Her example shows how professional pursuits can become a pathway to healing and empowerment.

## Reflections for the Reader

Take a thoughtful pause here. Savannah's story invites you to reflect on your own experiences with compassion and curiosity:

- ***Are there ways your past experiences influence how you view authority figures or how easily you extend trust?***

- ***Do you recognize coping behaviors that once helped you survive but now hold you back from thriving?***

- ***Who in your life could you safely confide in as a step toward releasing what you've carried alone?***

- ***What self-care practices, large or small, could you build into your daily routine to help you feel grounded and supported?***

________________________________________

________________________________________

________________________________________

________________________________________

Trauma does not dictate the future. It can, instead, become an invitation to redefine the path ahead and reconnect with ourselves. Your story matters, and your healing belongs to you. With every step toward honesty and self-compassion, you strengthen your ability to lead, connect, and live authentically.

Your next chapter awaits. Let's continue onward together.

CHAPTER 11

# Melissa's Story: Stepping out of the Shadows and into Her Trust

*"I'm still healing. I still have hard days. But I've learned healing doesn't require perfection; it requires honesty and compassion. My journey is ongoing, and I've finally learned to accept that with kindness toward myself."*

***—Melissa***

In sitting down with Melissa, I immediately sensed the resolve beneath her calm, thoughtful demeanor. At first glance, her accomplishments are striking: a thriving entrepreneur, dedicated mentor, and leader known for empowering others. Yet behind her poised exterior lies a deeply human journey marked by tremendous adversity and profound resilience.

Melissa's story, like those before, is one shaped by invisible wounds. Her trauma, deeply rooted in childhood, was severe and persistent, leaving emotional scars that lingered long into adulthood. Yet, in our conversation, I found myself inspired not only by her capacity to endure but by her remarkable transformation through intentional healing.

Melissa's experiences shine a necessary light on how unresolved trauma echoes throughout our lives, subtly influencing our health, relationships, and careers. Her reflections reveal a powerful truth: that facing our most painful memories with honesty, compassion, and courage can pave the way to reclaiming our lives in ways we once believed impossible.

In the following pages, Melissa will share her story, offering you a raw and honest glimpse into her experiences. I invite you to listen deeply, allowing her courage and vulnerability to resonate with you.

## Interview Dossier

**Name:** Melissa (pseudonym used to protect privacy)
**Age:** 37
**ACE Score:** 10 out of 10
**DISC Natural Style:** DI

## Background Snapshot

**Education:** Bachelor's degree
**Socioeconomic Background**: Middle-class upbringing
**Current Role:** Successful entrepreneur and business owner
**Years in the Working World:** Over 25 years
**Career Highlight:** Founding and leading a thriving business, recognized for mentoring and empowering other women entrepreneurs

## Trauma Timeline

**First Trauma:** Early childhood (age 3), severe emotional and physical abuse
**Duration of Abuse:** Persistent throughout childhood and adolescence
**Primary Abuser(s):** Mother and father
**Other Trauma:** Sexual abuse by multiple perpetrators, emotional and psychological neglect, severe bullying, and witnessing domestic violence
**Substance Use:** None

## Medical Conditions:

- Severe scoliosis (three significant back surgeries as a child)
- Ongoing chronic pain due to spinal issues and other health complications
- Struggles with anxiety and depression

Melissa sat down with me, radiating warmth and confidence that immediately filled the room. From our first moments speaking together, I felt a deep respect for the courage it took Melissa to share her experiences openly. Her presence was grounded, her voice steady yet charged with quiet strength.

As our conversation unfolded, Melissa opened up to me, sharing a world of memories that spanned a childhood filled with trauma and an adulthood dedicated to healing.

*"My earliest memories were painful. Both of my parents were deeply abusive—emotionally, physically, and psychologically. By the age of three, I had already learned to fear the very people who were supposed to protect me."*

Melissa's home, she explained, was unpredictable and unsafe, leaving her in a perpetual state of anxiety and fear.

At age six, Melissa experienced sexual abuse for the first time by a trusted family acquaintance. Like so many young victims, she never reported these incidents, carrying a heavy burden of shame and confusion.

*"I remember feeling frozen—trapped. I couldn't speak, couldn't cry out. That silence stayed with me for decades, becoming another weight I carried quietly."*

Throughout her childhood, Melissa experienced ongoing emotional abuse. Her father's anger often erupted violently, whereas her mother inflicted emotional cruelty, consistently criticizing her appearance, intelligence, and worth.

*"My mother's words cut deeper than anything. She would call me worthless, a disappointment, and tell me that no one would ever love me. After hearing that repeatedly, I believed her. Her voice became my internal voice, and it was devastating."*

Melissa's traumatic experiences extended beyond her family. Throughout her school years, she faced severe bullying, intensifying her sense of isolation and deepening her emotional wounds.

*"School was another battlefield. The bullying was relentless. I felt trapped—nowhere felt safe."*

Melissa's health became another source of trauma. At fourteen, she was diagnosed with severe scoliosis, requiring three extensive back surgeries that left her hospitalized for months. The chronic pain and physical limitations from these procedures continue to affect her today.

*"The surgeries were traumatic in themselves. I was isolated, scared, and in pain. It felt like another punishment I had to endure alone."*

Melissa's adolescence included further struggles: sexual violence by partners, an abusive first marriage marked by emotional and verbal abuse, and the loss of her father to cancer when she was only twenty-three.

Each trauma compounded the next, yet Melissa quietly carried these burdens alone, believing she had no other choice.

Despite immense adversity, Melissa found a turning point in her mid-thirties when she initiated therapy. Initially seeking marriage counseling, she soon realized she needed individual therapy. Therapy became a powerful catalyst, allowing her to face and unpack her long-standing traumas for the first time.

*"Therapy was transformative. It was the first time someone validated my experiences. I learned my trauma wasn't my fault, and I began to reclaim my identity."*

In therapy, Melissa began to confront and rewrite her internal narrative. She developed healthier coping skills, actively practiced journaling, gratitude exercises, and mindfulness to manage her emotional health. Her therapist helped her recognize patterns stemming from trauma, particularly around perfectionism, trust, and self-worth.

At age forty, Melissa took a profound step forward: She became an entrepreneur. Starting her own business gave her a sense of purpose, independence, and confidence she had never known before.

*"Entrepreneurship gave me my voice back. It taught me to trust myself, my instincts, and my ability to lead. I discovered I could succeed on my terms—not for external validation but because I knew I deserved success."*

Today, Melissa's thriving business serves as more than a professional achievement. It has become a platform for mentoring other women, advocating openly for trauma-informed support in the business sector, and guiding others toward healing. Melissa's work empowers her and those around her, translating her experiences into wisdom and strength.

She acknowledges her journey is far from over. Healing, she explains, is not a linear process. Melissa still faces daily challenges, chronic pain, and emotional hurdles. Yet she emphasizes the power of authenticity and grace.

*"I'm still healing. I still have hard days. But I've learned healing doesn't require perfection—it requires honesty and compassion. My journey is ongoing, and I've finally learned to accept that with kindness toward myself."*

Melissa defines healing clearly and powerfully:

*"Healing, to me, means living fully in the present without constant fear. It means quieting that internal critic, releasing the shame that was never mine to carry, and finding joy in who I am today."*

Melissa's journey is a testament to the transformative power of courage, intentionality, and self-compassion. Her story illuminates clearly how deeply trauma can shape our lives and yet how profoundly we can reclaim and rewrite our narratives when we choose authenticity and healing.

## What We Can Learn from Melissa's Journey

Melissa's story highlights how deeply trauma can shape identity and self-worth, yet also how courage and intentional choices can rewrite the narrative. Her life shows that healing is not about erasing the past but about reclaiming power in everyday ways—through work, relationships, and self-compassion.

**Rebuilding Self-worth from Within:** Years of abuse left Melissa doubting her value. By naming those experiences and confronting the lies she had internalized, she learned to create a healthier inner voice. Her journey reminds us that part of healing is choosing whose voices we carry forward—and whose we release.

**Creating New Narratives through Work:** Entrepreneurship gave Melissa more than a livelihood. It became the space where she discovered her capability, leadership, and purpose on her own terms. For many survivors, professional courage is tied to personal recovery, opening doors to confidence and independence that trauma once tried to take away.

**Healing through Consistency:** Melissa's progress hasn't come from a single breakthrough moment but from steady practices—therapy, mindfulness, journaling, and small daily rituals. Her story affirms that lasting growth often happens in the quiet, ordinary choices we make every day.

Melissa's life is proof that although trauma may leave lasting marks, it does not get the final word. With honesty, support, and persistence, we can choose to reclaim ourselves and create a future defined by strength and intention.

## Reflections for the Reader

Take a moment to reflect on Melissa's journey and how it connects to your own:

- ***How have the words or beliefs of others shaped the way you see yourself, and which of those voices deserve to be released?***

___

___

___

___

- ***In what ways could your work or professional life become a place of healing, confidence, or purpose?***

___

___

___

___

- ***What small, consistent practices help you feel steady and grounded when challenges resurface?***

____________________

____________________

____________________

____________________

- ***How can you begin to define your worth apart from external validation or the opinions of others?***

____________________

____________________

____________________

____________________

Melissa's story reminds us that healing often happens step by step in our daily choices to believe in our value, create new patterns, and live into our worth. Your past may have left its mark, but it does not decide your future. Each intentional step you take holds power.

Your story matters. And your next chapter is waiting.

CHAPTER 12

# When Trauma Meets Partnership: Melissa and Savannah's Business Journey

*"Knowing yourself is the beginning of all wisdom."*

***—Aristotle***

When I sat down separately with Melissa and Savannah, I immediately understood that their partnership was more than a business venture; it was a genuine connection. Here were two profoundly resilient women, both with significant trauma backgrounds, deliberately choosing to build something meaningful together. Both Melissa and Savannah had shared openly and candidly about their individual journeys—Savannah's quiet strength and cautious communication style shaped by childhood instability and Melissa's bold assertiveness, rooted in a past that demanded constant vigilance and self-defense.

What struck me most was how clearly each of them acknowledged their trauma-informed approach to work despite the fact that each interview had taken place separately. It became evident to me that their partnership was rooted in a shared awareness, both of themselves and each other, despite their distinct personalities and backgrounds.

Each woman had clearly outlined to me how trauma influenced their professional behavior. Melissa described herself as blunt and direct, explaining openly: *"I'm not a great communicator because of my trauma—the way my tonality sometimes turns people off, and it's not intentional."* She understood that her trauma led her to communicate in ways that unintentionally alienated others. Savannah, on the other hand, described her trauma as making her cautious, conflict-avoidant, and hesitant to speak up. She was hyperaware of criticism, remaining overly sensitive to negative feedback and prone to withdrawing during tense moments. These vastly different styles created ongoing conflict and difficulty between them. Recognizing this challenge, they wisely sought executive coaching together to better understand and relate to one another. Initially, both women doubted whether they could continue to collaborate effectively, but after completing DISC assessments, their interpersonal dynamics and DISC behavioral patterns became clearer. With these new insights, we were finally able to work through their differences, helping them develop healthier communication patterns and improved understanding.

What I found remarkable was the deliberate, careful approach each took to navigating these patterns. Melissa acknowledged openly that her instinct to control outcomes was a coping mechanism born from childhood chaos and unpredictability: *"My walls go up, and I go into battle mode when I feel attacked."* Savannah, in contrast, shared with me how she instinctively withdrew from confrontation, admitting: *"I felt trapped—nowhere felt safe,"* a feeling that had continued to affect her adult interactions.

Their partnership offered something both had rarely experienced before: safety. Each had described to me the deep fear ingrained by their early trauma, and yet both had consciously chosen to trust each other in building a professional relationship. Although their interviews didn't specifically detail exact conversations between them, each woman explicitly described using their trauma-informed understanding to manage their interactions better.

For example, Melissa described intentionally practicing patience and moderation in her responses at work. She shared that becoming aware of how her assertiveness could be perceived as abrasive had changed the way she approached conflicts professionally. Savannah openly acknowledged her practice of carefully communicating her emotional state when triggered or stressed, explaining that this transparency was necessary for her own emotional safety and professional effectiveness. These individual strategies clearly suggest a mutual dynamic built on emotional awareness and intentional communication, which are critical for a trauma-informed partnership.

They both explicitly emphasized the importance of self-awareness for professional success. Savannah, reflecting upon her professional journey, stated clearly: *"Healing, to me, means being able to fully enjoy life's moments without constantly fearing the worst. It means quieting that internal voice that always says, 'What if?' and learning to live in the now."* Melissa similarly spoke clearly about her ongoing healing process and professional evolution: *"Healing, to me, means living fully in the present without constant fear. It means quieting that internal critic, releasing the shame that was never mine to carry, and finding joy in who I am today."* Their individual articulations of healing were strikingly similar, reflecting how trauma-informed practices had been foundational for each woman's professional growth.

As an observer, it was clear that their partnership likely amplified each of their personal strengths. Savannah's natural empathy, clearly shaped by her own history of neglect and emotional pain, combined powerfully with Melissa's bold determination to speak openly and take charge, itself clearly born from a childhood of having to assert herself to survive. Their complementary strengths, rooted in their individual coping mechanisms, likely created an effective balance in decision-making, leadership, and day-to-day operations.

Each woman independently expressed to me the critical role of intentional self-care and emotional management in their personal and professional routines. Melissa described clearly her daily journaling practice, mindfulness, and gratitude exercises as essential tools for emotional resilience. Savannah similarly articulated the centrality of daily self-care in her routine, explicitly citing journaling, gratitude exercises, mindfulness practices, and regular therapy sessions. Their shared dedication to these emotional strategies undoubtedly strengthened their ability to work effectively together despite personal triggers or stresses.

Their partnership also clearly demonstrated the need to redefine success internally. Both women, driven early in their lives by external validation as a means of compensating for deep-seated feelings of inadequacy and rejection, had arrived at a clear understanding that genuine success must come from within. Melissa reflected openly on how entrepreneurship had become a powerful vehicle for reclaiming her voice and establishing self-confidence independent of external validation. Savannah similarly expressed that entrepreneurship represented a reclaiming of her own narrative and professional confidence separate from past definitions imposed by trauma or external expectations.

In their respective interviews, each woman expressed clearly how their professional journey served as a pathway to healing. For Savannah, starting her own business was not merely a career choice but an empowering act of self-discovery, allowing her to rewrite her internal narrative about self-worth and capability, sharing, *"I was really freaking proud of myself, and it was the first time that I didn't need anybody else to be proud of me."* Melissa clearly described entrepreneurship as a transformative way to reclaim personal power and agency, stating openly, *"The more that I was growing in my career ... that gave me a backbone."*

When considering these two individuals working together, it was clear that their partnership was more than a professional collaboration—it was a mutual support in the ongoing journey of healing and evolution. Each clearly recognized the role of authenticity and self-compassion, openly discussing the necessity of being gentle with themselves as they navigated their professional roles and relationships. Neither claimed to have completed their healing journey; rather, each explicitly emphasized the ongoing nature of healing and self-improvement.

Their clearly articulated reflections on trauma-informed awareness in the professional setting provide us, the readers, valuable and actionable lessons. Savannah's and Melissa's individual stories demonstrate explicitly the power of recognizing trauma's impact on communication, trust, decision-making, and leadership. Their clear dedication to creating a trauma-informed workplace illustrates that empathy, vulnerability, and emotional safety are not only personal values but essential professional practices. Their partnership exemplifies the idea that trauma-informed collaboration can transform challenges into strengths and past trauma into powerful lessons for authentic leadership and effective communication.

## Reflections for the Reader

Take a moment to consider how Melissa's and Savannah's partnership might speak to your own professional life:

- ***In what ways have your past experiences shaped how you communicate, trust, or collaborate with others?***

____________________________________________

____________________________________________

____________________________________________

____________________________________________

- ***Are there coping strategies you've outgrown that now hold you back at work or in leadership? What healthier approaches could take their place?***

____________________________________________

____________________________________________

____________________________________________

____________________________________________

- *How might you begin to build more trauma-aware practices in your team or workplace—through empathy, transparency, or creating safety in conversations?*

- *What would it mean for you to define success on your own terms, rooted in confidence and clarity rather than external approval?*

- *Who in your circle feels safe enough to share your story with—someone who can listen without judgment and walk with you in your growth?*

Melissa's and Savannah's stories show that healing and leadership do not happen separately. They are intertwined. By choosing to face the past with honesty and grace, they remind us that our histories can become a foundation for deeper connection, stronger leadership, and more authentic success.

# CHAPTER 13

# Margot's Story: Reclaiming Safety and Finding Self-worth

*"I don't have to let my past define my future. Each step forward gives me the confidence to keep moving forward. Each step is a reclamation of myself."*

***—Margot***

As I sat down with Margot, I was immediately drawn to the sincerity in her voice and the thoughtful way she approached our conversation. At thirty-four, Margot is an insightful, compassionate, and quietly determined entrepreneur, yet her composed exterior belies the deep and ongoing struggles resulting from childhood trauma.

Margot's story is significant because it clearly demonstrates how even a relatively low ACE score can have profound, lasting effects on a person's life. With an ACE score of two, she underscores that the depth of trauma's impact isn't necessarily measured by its numeric severity but rather by the emotional wounds and long-lasting repercussions it leaves behind.

## Interview Dossier

**Name:** Margot (pseudonym used to protect privacy)
**Age:** 34
**ACE Score:** 2 out of 10
**DISC Natural Style:** Cs

## Background Snapshot

**Education:** Bachelor's degree
**Socioeconomic Background:** Middle-class upbringing
**Current Role:** Founder and CEO of a fast-growing company
**Years in the Working World:** Over 10 years
**Career Highlight:** Building a successful and stable company from the ground up, gaining recognition and respect in her professional community

## Trauma Timeline

**First Trauma:** Early childhood, ongoing emotional and physical abuse
**Duration of Abuse:** Persistent throughout childhood and adolescence
**Primary Abuser(s):** Mother
**Other Trauma:** Severe emotional manipulation, intense fear, and chronic anxiety, combined with severe instability in the home
**Substance Use:** None

## Medical Conditions:

- Anxiety disorder and persistent burnout linked directly to unresolved childhood trauma
- Chronic fatigue resulting from emotional stress and overworking
- History of significant weight fluctuations resulting in gastric sleeve surgery

From the start of our conversation, Margot spoke candidly about her childhood environment, which was marked by persistent emotional instability and fear, primarily from her mother.

*"I never really felt safe as a child,"* she explained clearly. *"There were stages when the consequence was being physically hit. So, I think, from an early age, I developed a strong fear of making mistakes."*

Margot grew up in a deeply religious and controlling household, which she described as having cult-like elements. Her mother's strict adherence to a harsh interpretation of religious doctrines severely affected Margot's sense of safety and self-worth.

*"I always had this recurring dream where I lose everything for whatever reason, and I'm back in that spot—I'm stuck and "I'm scared and I have nowhere to go,"* she shared with me candidly. These unresolved fears followed her into adulthood, manifesting as anxiety-driven behaviors and an obsessive need for stability and control.

Margot's childhood was shaped by a complicated relationship with her mother, who not only administered physical punishment but also consistently undermined Margot's sense of self-worth. The emotional manipulation was severe, characterized by confusing contradictions that left Margot constantly doubting herself.

*"My mom would always say, 'No one will ever believe you.' And so, I learned to stay silent,"* Margot told me, her voice filled with a quiet power that clearly underscored her acceptance of her past struggle. *"I felt invisible, unimportant. There was never emotional safety. I was always trying to be perfect, to earn validation that never came."*

Margot's trauma clearly influenced her behavioral style, particularly in her professional life. Her DISC natural style is C/S—Cautious and Steady. Her intense need to analyze, double-check, and constantly second-guess decisions stems directly from the fear and uncertainty ingrained in her early life.

*"Inside, there's always this anxiety,"* Margot explained candidly. *"I'm constantly overthinking because there's a fear of making mistakes. I need everything to be perfect because that's what safety felt like to me."*

This perfectionism became an exhausting cycle of overwork and burnout. Margot candidly shared that her inability to stop working, her need for constant productivity, was rooted in her past trauma. *"There's safety in always working,"* she acknowledged openly. *"It's like I'm constantly trying to build a fortress around me, but it leads to burnout."*

Margot's trauma manifested physically as well, most notably through significant struggles with her weight. She revealed that she had undergone a gastric sleeve surgery procedure to remove 90% of her stomach, a fact she seldom discusses. Her weight struggles were deeply tied to her emotional trauma as her body became a physical manifestation of the unresolved emotional pain she carried for years.

Her healing journey began with therapy, an essential step she took to confront her past. Margot candidly shared that therapy allowed her to recognize the trauma-informed patterns driving her anxiety, perfectionism, and burnout. Her therapist helped her begin to understand the deeper root causes of her fears, behaviors, and self-sabotage.

*"Therapy has been transformative,"* Margot reflected clearly. *"It's the first time someone has helped me truly see and validate my experiences."*

In addition to therapy, Margot emphasized the crucial role of community and emotional support in her healing journey. She expressed clearly how finding safe spaces and supportive relationships allowed her to begin reclaiming her voice and building genuine self-worth.

*"I now have people who cheer me on,"* she shared openly. *"For the first time, I feel like I can trust people. They're telling me, 'You can do this.' And I'm starting to believe it."*

Margot's entrepreneurial journey became another essential element of her healing process. Starting her own company was a way for her to regain control, build safety, and prove her capabilities to herself. Entrepreneurship allowed her to challenge her ingrained fear and assert her true self.

*"Starting my own company has forced me to trust myself more,"* Margot explained candidly. *"It's scary, but it's also empowering. It's helping me reclaim parts of myself that I felt were beaten out of me."*

As our conversation concluded, Margot made it clear that her healing journey was ongoing and that she didn't follow an easily replicable path. Yet, despite setbacks and struggles, she clearly articulated the profound value of self-awareness and intentional healing.

*"Healing means that I no longer have to live in fear,"* she said clearly. *"I don't have to let my past define my future. Each step forward gives me the confidence to keep moving forward. Each step is a reclamation of myself."*

Margot's courage, openness, and resilience clearly demonstrated that healing is possible even from deeply ingrained wounds. Her story vividly illustrates how unresolved trauma can shape our professional and personal behaviors and how confronting our past with honesty and compassion can transform pain into strength and purpose.

## What We Can Learn from Margot's Journey:

**Trauma Is Not Defined by Severity Alone:** Margot's relatively low ACE score underscores that the depth of trauma's impact is emotional, not numeric. Even a seemingly small number of traumatic experiences can profoundly shape one's emotional health and professional identity.

**Perfectionism as Trauma Response:** Margot's intense need for perfection, driven by childhood fear and uncertainty, highlights how perfectionism can become a damaging coping mechanism rather than a beneficial trait.

**Importance of Emotional Safety:** Her story clearly emphasizes the profound importance of emotional safety and validation in childhood, illustrating the lasting damage caused when emotional safety is absent.

**Entrepreneurship as Empowerment:** Starting her business became Margot's pathway to reclaiming her voice and building a sense of control and safety previously unattainable.

**Community and Therapy are Essential:** Margot's healing clearly demonstrates the crucial role of supportive relationships and professional therapy in overcoming trauma.

## Reflections for the Reader:

- ***When has striving for excellence crossed into exhaustion or self-criticism for you?***

___

___

___

___

- ***What would it look like to value progress over perfection in your daily work or relationships?***

___

___

___

___

- ***Have you ever tied your sense of worth to accomplishments? How might you begin to define your value apart from achievement?***

---

---

---

---

- ***What simple boundary or self-kindness could you practice this week to honor your well-being instead of overextending yourself?***

---

---

---

---

Margot's story is a reminder that the urge to overachieve is not always ambition—it can be a survival strategy. By naming it and seeking support, she began to loosen its grip and step into authenticity. Her journey demonstrates that true strength is found in the courage to be genuine.

Your story, too, is yours to claim and reshape proudly. The past may have left its mark, but it does not decide your future.

## CHAPTER 14

# Jane's Story: A Silent Struggle

*"Taking the first step is the hardest. Each step after that builds a walkway carrying you toward a life in which you can experience real purpose and freedom."*

***—Jane***

In this chapter, we explore a different perspective—a powerful reminder that the impact of trauma isn't always correlated directly with its numerical severity. I sat down with Jane, a thoughtful and insightful woman, who shared with me how profoundly her experience had shaped her entire life.

Jane is fifty years old, recently retired from a successful career in business, and notably has an ACE score of only one. On paper, it might seem minor compared to some of the stories we've heard, yet her experience demonstrates that even a short but traumatic period of life can have lifelong repercussions if left unresolved. Jane's journey illustrates how trauma—no matter the scale—can silently infiltrate our lives, influencing our professional identities, emotional health, and self-worth in subtle yet devastating ways.

Jane agreed to share her story, albeit cautiously and without divulging specifics, in hopes of encouraging others who might be carrying similar burdens silently. For decades, she buried what had happened, believing that silence was safer. Yet that silence became its own form of prison—fueling shame, self-doubt, and a persistent feeling of being unworthy.

The weight of her unresolved trauma and the shame surrounding it profoundly shaped her professional and personal path. Her decision to finally seek help became a transformative act of reclaiming her voice, her dignity, and ultimately, her life.

Take your time with Jane's words. Allow her honesty and vulnerability to speak deeply to your own experiences and reflections.

## Interview Dossier

**Name:** Jane (pseudonym used to protect privacy)
**Age:** 50
**ACE Score:** 1 out of 10
**DISC Natural Style:** D

## Background Snapshot

**Education:** Bachelor's degree
**Socioeconomic Background:** Middle-class upbringing
**Current Role:** Retired, previously successful in the business world
**Years in the Working World:** Over 25 years
**Career Highlight:** Consistently recognized for overachievement and dedication, driven by the hidden need for validation

## Trauma Timeline

**First and Primary Trauma:** In early adulthood, I had several abortions resulting from serious relationships, compounded by a lack of emotional support and resources
**Duration of Impact:** Lifelong, until addressed through therapy later in life
**Other Trauma:** Emotional neglect during childhood, feelings of isolation and abandonment
**Substance Use:** None reported

## Medical Conditions:

- Chronic emotional distress manifesting as anxiety, depression, and suicidal thoughts
- Intense self-loathing and perfectionism resulting from unresolved trauma

When I sat down with Jane, I could immediately sense her quiet dignity and emotional depth. On the surface, she radiates an image of polished success, hard work, and accomplishment. Yet, behind these impressive achievements was a hidden narrative of pain and self-condemnation that she carried privately for decades.

Jane agreed to share her story with me cautiously, emphasizing that she wasn't yet ready to reveal every detail. She told me clearly that her motivation in speaking out was simple: "*Living with unaddressed trauma and the burden of shame and guilt has had a corrosive and devastating effect on my life. If sharing my story encourages someone to seek help, it was worth telling.*"

Jane grew up in a troubled home characterized by emotional neglect. Despite external appearances, she was immature. She was sheltered and totally unprepared to enter college and young adulthood. "*I was hardworking and well educated,*" she explained, "*but I was extremely immature emotionally.*"

By her early twenties, Jane had already experienced several serious relationships that resulted in several pregnancies and subsequent abortions. While choosing not to delve into specific details, Jane revealed the profound emotional toll these decisions took on her. "*The trauma that resulted from those few tumultuous years has been immense,*" she confided. The stigma and silence surrounding abortion left her feeling completely isolated without any resources or safe spaces to seek support. "*Even if I wanted to get help, where was the self-help group for people who had abortions?*" she asked poignantly.

And when I asked her why she never sought therapy, her response was: *"No one could possibly have been as irresponsible as I was, and my story is just too bad to share. I made the decisions I made to protect my family from any shame. I didn't have anyone in my life at that time with whom I could safely share."*

*"I had no emotional support. Furthermore, I felt that I deserved to bear all that shame as a consequence of my actions. So, I've worn the guilt and the shame for my entire life with no relief. The static from the tapes of guilt and shame that run constantly in my head is always there."*

Her unresolved trauma manifested powerfully in her professional life. Driven relentlessly by a desperate need for validation, Jane became an obsessive overachiever. She viewed herself as a fair boss but a bit unattached. She expected a lot from her employees, but she didn't give much praise. Her mask was always fully attached with no vulnerability ever shown. Her career was marked by an insatiable pursuit of perfection, a craving for external affirmation that she now describes vividly:

*"The accolades were my drug, and I worked even harder to stay on top. I had no off button, no off ramp, no ability to say no. My relentless hard work was an attempt to prove my self-worth. Period. I had none."*

Yet beneath her successful exterior was a constant current of self-loathing and emotional exhaustion. Jane candidly described living with her internal critic that fueled her perfectionism: *"Just keep running, just keep juggling, just keep smiling. It will be OK. You can manage it. You've got this,"* she would tell herself, masking her deep emptiness and shame.

Jane's life looked picture-perfect from the outside, but inwardly she was weighed down by guilt and shame from her earlier decisions, which she viewed through a harsh and unforgiving lens. *"My outside life bore no resemblance to the scared, scarred, and shamed woman living on the inside,"* she confessed. Although she could readily forgive others for youthful mistakes, she could not grant herself the same grace.

This hidden emotional burden continued to build until it reached a critical breaking point during an unexpected personal crisis. At that moment, decades of suppressed pain surged forth, resulting in what Jane described as *"a mental breakdown."* Recognizing the gravity of her situation, Jane confided in one person, who immediately understood the severity of her pain and connected her to professional help. *"This referral literally changed my life,"* she emphasized, reflecting on this pivotal moment.

Therapy became Jane's lifeline. She recounted her initial sessions vividly: *"I assured [my therapist] that my story would surely be the worst story she had ever heard."* Yet through therapy, she learned to explore the root of her emotional wounds and identified deeply ingrained patterns from childhood that contributed to her trauma. She realized that the true trauma was not only the events themselves but also the profound lack of support and emotional safety at crucial junctures of her life.

Over the course of several months of intensive work with her therapist, Jane discovered the transformative power of compassion for her younger self. She explained how therapy helped her separate responsibility for her past choices from the crushing burden of shame and self-condemnation. *"I learned that I could take responsibility for my actions and, at the same time, have compassion and forgiveness for myself. I could love myself in spite of what I had done."*

Jane openly expressed regret for having waited so long to seek help. She shared this reflection with profound clarity:

*"Had I understood how life-changing it would be to experience true healing, I would have pursued therapy long ago. I was fixated on the idea that my story was so shocking, so on the fringe, that no one would understand it. I believed my punishment was to be forever burdened with thick layers of guilt."*

Today, Jane passionately encourages others who may be silently carrying trauma to seek support. Her message is clear and powerful: *"Taking the first step is the hardest. Each step after that builds a walkway carrying you toward a life in which you can experience real purpose and freedom."*

Jane's journey is a compelling testament to the immense value of seeking help, even when it seems impossible to confront past pain. She reminds us that trauma is not defined by quantity or scale but by the depth of its emotional impact. Even a single traumatic event, left unaddressed, can profoundly shape our emotional health, self-worth, and professional identities.

Her story highlights the crucial importance of emotional safety and support, not only in childhood but throughout life. Jane urges readers to recognize that healing is available and that isolation born of shame can be broken. Her willingness to share, even cautiously and with careful boundaries, sends a powerful message of hope, resilience, and the possibility of reclaiming one's life.

## What We Can Learn from Jane's Story:

Jane's story reveals how easily pain can be underestimated when it doesn't fit our cultural idea of "serious trauma." Her experience challenges the notion that suffering must be visible or extreme to be valid. It shows how silence and self-judgment can deepen the wound long after the event itself has passed—and how the simple act of seeking help can become a turning point toward freedom.

**No Trauma Is Too Small:** Jane's story powerfully demonstrates that trauma is not measured by the number of adverse events experienced but by the emotional toll those experiences take. Her story reminds us that even one short traumatic period in life can create lifelong wounds if left unresolved. Recognizing and validating all trauma, regardless of how it compares to others' experiences, is vital for healing.

**The Hidden Costs of Silence:** Jane spent decades carrying emotional burdens in silence, fearing judgment and rejection. Her journey reveals clearly that shame and isolation can magnify trauma's impact. Speaking even to a single person was transformative for her, underscoring the immense power in breaking silence.

**Overachievement as a Mask for Pain:** Jane's relentless pursuit of perfection and professional success masked a deeper emotional void. Her story reveals a common coping strategy for trauma survivors: external validation through high achievement. Understanding that success and self-worth must be defined from within is crucial for healing.

**Compassion as a Healing Tool**: Through therapy, Jane learned the profound importance of extending compassion toward herself, especially her younger self who lacked support. Recognizing her need for compassion enabled her to release shame, opening a path toward genuine self-acceptance and forgiveness.

**Healing Requires Courage and Authenticity**: Jane's healing journey began when she finally confronted her pain directly. Her experience highlights the courage required to face trauma honestly and seek support. She emphasizes that healing isn't about perfection; it is about authenticity, openness, and a willingness to engage deeply with past pain to reclaim the present.

## Reflections for the Reader

Pause thoughtfully, and consider Jane's insights:

- ***Have you ever told yourself your experience "wasn't bad enough" or conversely, was "so bad" you were ashamed to seek support?***

________________________________________

________________________________________

________________________________________

________________________________________

- ***Where do you still confuse taking responsibility with carrying lifelong punishment? What might it look like to set that burden down?***

- ***In what ways have you relied on achievement or productivity to quiet an inner critic? What could you use instead to affirm your worth?***

- ***Who is one safe person you could talk to about what you've carried alone, and what would you ask of them?***

- ***What simple practice could help you cultivate self-forgiveness this month (e.g., a brief letter to your younger self, a weekly check-in, or one compassionate boundary)?***

---

---

---

---

Jane's journey powerfully reminds us that healing is possible for everyone, no matter the details or size of our past trauma. Your story, whatever it includes, matters deeply— and every intentional step you take toward healing brings you closer to reclaiming your true self and your right to live fully.

# CHAPTER 15

# Reggie's Story: Transforming Pain into Purpose

*"Pain to passion. Passion to purpose. Purpose to power. Power to peace. That is the process of perseverance."*

***—Reggie D. Ford***

When I sat down with Reggie, I immediately sensed our conversation would hold a unique depth. His experiences differed from many others I'd spoken with primarily due to the continuous and complex nature of his trauma, which began in childhood and continues to require active management today.

As an African American man, Reggie gently highlighted the significance of culturally nuanced healing without allowing it to overshadow the universal themes of resilience and recovery. Yet, like so many others, he discovered entrepreneurship as a critical pathway toward reclaiming personal agency, rebuilding self-worth, and finding profound meaning in his healing journey. Hearing Reggie's thoughtful reflections provided invaluable insights, reminding me of the importance of understanding and embracing the full spectrum of human experiences, especially those outside our own.

## Interview Dossier

**Name:** Reggie D. Ford (*real name used with permission*)
**Age:** 34
**ACE Score:** 10 out of 10
**DISC Natural Style:** CD

## Background Snapshot

**Education:** Bachelor's degree in economics and corporate strategy; Master's of Accountancy; currently pursuing a Master's of Applied Positive Psychology at the University of Pennsylvania
**Socioeconomic Background:** Low socioeconomic status
**Current Role:** Wellness and resilience architect, entrepreneur, wealth advisor, author, speaker, certified yoga instructor
**Years in the Working World:** 11 years
**Career Highlight:** Founding RoseCrete Wealth Management; recognized author and speaker passionately advocating for mental health and resilience

## Trauma Timeline

**First and Primary Trauma:** From birth onward; severe emotional neglect, abandonment, and complex trauma involving emotional and verbal abuse primarily from mother and maternal grandmother, abandonment by father, and sexual abuse beginning around age three or four

**Duration of Impact:** Lifelong, ongoing, currently managed through therapy and active personal healing practices

**Other Trauma:** Continuous emotional cruelty and verbal abuse through adulthood from family, persistent feelings of isolation and abandonment, racialized trauma, and witnessing acute community violence

**Substance Use:** None

## Medical Conditions:

- Complex PTSD linked directly to prolonged childhood trauma
- Chronic anxiety and depression manifesting from unresolved trauma
- Hypertension and high cholesterol (improved significantly through dietary changes and holistic wellness practices)
- History of severe emotional distress and challenges with self-sabotaging behaviors stemming from trauma responses

At thirty-four, Reggie has already built an impressive career as a wellness and resilience architect, entrepreneur, wealth advisor, certified yoga instructor, author, and speaker. Yet, beneath these professional accolades lies a compelling and ongoing story of overcoming complex trauma and channeling his pain into purpose. Reggie described his early emotional landscape vividly: *"My emotions were muted because that was part of my safety. The only emotion I really remember experiencing as a child was rage. It was acceptable for a boy to show anger but not sadness or fear."* He recalled sexual abuse starting around age three or four, an experience he never reported and silently carried for decades. His mother and maternal grandmother's emotional cruelty further compounded his trauma, creating an environment in which trauma was normalized.

His father's absence created additional abandonment wounds. *"My dad is more neglect. ... He wasn't really there,"* Reggie explained. Despite these adversities, his strength came through his paternal grandparents—his *"soul parents." "The number one factor in building resilience is having at least one loving, caring, supportive adult, and I had two,"* Reggie shared.

Today, Reggie speaks candidly about this history on stages across the country, where he has become a sought-after motivational speaker and advocate for mental health and resilience. As the best-selling author of *Perseverance through Severe Dysfunction,* he reframes PTSD as "Perseverance through Severe Dysfunction" and shares his message that trauma need not define a life—it can instead be transformed into passion, purpose, power, and ultimately peace.

I had the pleasure of meeting Reggie when he delivered the keynote for our annual Healing Housing luncheon. I was blown away by his sheer power of personality and his ability to connect with his audience. He left us spellbound with his piercing delivery of his life story and how he overcame immense adversity. He is incredibly smart, witty, and captivating. As I wiped my tears and approached the stage after he completed his talk, I could barely speak. I shook his hand, thanked him, and asked if I could contact him regarding a project I was working on. I knew in that moment that I had to tell his story as part of this book.

In addition to his work as the founder of RoseCrete Wealth Management, Reggie serves on multiple nonprofit boards focused on health care, wellness, and childhood empowerment. His insights have been featured in *Forbes*, *ESPN*, and *USA Today*, further amplifying his mission to inspire others to embrace vulnerability, confront trauma, and pursue a more fulfilling life of peace and abundance.

Professionally, Reggie recognized the dual impact of trauma. Although mistrust and self-sabotage posed significant challenges, his experiences also honed his deep empathy and understanding of others. "*My trauma deeply impacted my interpersonal relationships. It's very difficult to build relationships when I don't feel trust or safety,*" he admitted. Yet he also noted, "*I don't feel comfortable connecting with people, but I can, and I do it really well ... because of my experience.*"

Entrepreneurship emerged as a pathway to reclaim control: "*Starting my own business provided independence and confidence. ... It gave me my voice back.*"

Addressing race and mental health stigma, Reggie highlighted deep-seated cultural perceptions: "*Therapy is for White people. ... If we saw someone going to therapy, it wasn't a Black person.*" His own initial dismissal by a doctor further emphasized the importance of culturally competent care: *"I talked to my primary care physician. ... he waved me off. ... I kept advocating for myself. I got a new doctor ... culturally appropriate. ... She understood that Black men aren't as vulnerable in that way."*

Reggie pursued extensive therapeutic support, including trauma therapy, EMDR, CBT, neurofeedback, yoga, meditation, and mindfulness, significantly reducing the intensity and duration of his emotional triggers. He openly acknowledged the financial privilege required for such care and expressed gratitude for opportunities like the scholarship he received for a retreat at ONSITE.

Located in Tennessee with an additional campus in California, ONSITE is a nationally recognized wellness organization offering immersive therapeutic retreats, outpatient programs, and online courses designed to help people heal from trauma, reduce stress, and reconnect with themselves. Programs such as the Living Centered Program, trauma healing intensives, equine therapy, and nature-based adventures blend evidence-based clinical approaches with restorative hospitality. ONSITE also operates an intensive outpatient program in Nashville and custom-designed intensives for individuals, couples, and families. Their mission is to create transformative spaces that foster emotional wellness, growth, and lasting personal change.

His reflections on psychological safety underscore its essential role in healing: *"Psychological safety is the ability to be vulnerable, take risks, and be yourself without fear of repercussion. ... It's needed in moments of trauma and growth."*

At the close of our conversation, Reggie offered powerful wisdom: *"The pain of healing is worth the peace it brings. Healing is not linear—it requires honesty, compassion, and intentionality. It's an ongoing journey, transforming pain into profound purpose."*

He then shared an original poem, *"Today Is the Day,"* capturing his journey toward healing:

# "Today is the Day"

## by Reggie Ford

It's about time to **change your ways.**
You've been saying **tomorrow is the day** for far too many days.
How many moons must go by before you begin to see
That your **actions of today** will result in the person you want to be?
Insanity, they say, is doing the same thing but expecting
something different.
But no, no not you - you want to be **magnificent**
A word in Latin that means **great deeds.**
But somehow you keep getting bogged down in the weeds.
**It's time today** to change your ways.
To **commit to the process,** even on the days it doesn't pay.
Even on the days **that it rains**
Even on the days **full of pain**
Even on the days **you feel sick**
You don't deviate from the standard. Because that's the whole meaning
behind the words **"I commit."**
It's time to **lock in,** because you deserve your best.
**Others can't cheat you of success,**
because only you were given your test.
**Ace it** for all the broken hearts and aces.
**Ace it** for the deep scars and smiling faces.
**Ace it** because you, my friend, are destined for greatness.
You've got everything that you need to **accomplish the goal.**
The only thing holding you back is the person you're afraid to get to know.
**Look yourself in the mirror** and be real with your reflection.
You hate rejection, denial, criticism, and objection.
**You love praise,** and the pleasure you get from external validation.
You like standing ovations from **your words of inspiration.**
You fear uncertainty, but know that in every situation
When you gave it your all, you exceeded your **wildest expectations**.
So step aside, old self, stop getting in the way.
Yesterday, you said tomorrow, **so today is the day.**

Reggie concluded with empathy toward his abusers: *"I have tremendous grace, respect, understanding, and love for those who may have abused me. ... I recognize the pain they caused was a result of their own pain."*

His story, however, does not end with mere survival—it is about transformation and leadership. Through his book, *Perseverance through Severe Dysfunction: Breaking the Curse of Intergenerational Trauma as a Black Man in America* (2021), Reggie has given voice to countless others who feel silenced by trauma. The book has been praised for its raw honesty, courageous vulnerability, and insistence that immense suffering can be converted into improbable success. By reframing PTSD as "Perseverance through Severe Dysfunction," he has expanded the conversation about trauma recovery in both clinical and cultural spaces, helping normalize dialogue on mental health, especially within communities of color.

## From *PTSD,* he closes with the following sage advice:

> *"In closing, our time on Earth is as short, in the grand scheme of things, as the dash between our birth and death dates on our tombstone. That dash represents everything that you did in life. Your successes and your failures. Take advantage of every moment in life, and leave a lasting impact. Make the world a better place because you were a part of it.*
>
> *No matter your background, life will challenge every cell in your body. You will face obstacles, and you will be tested to overcome the most difficult challenges. The difficulties in life won't get any easier the longer you live, but you will get stronger. You may bend, but you won't break.*
>
> *Your trauma does not define you. While you will always carry the nightmares of your past, you don't have to let them affect your dreams. Everything that you have gone through has helped shape you into the person that you are. Good, bad,*

*or indifferent—it's a part of you. You never completely get over your trauma. You continue to live with it. Even then, it can have one of two effects on you: It can break you, or it can make you stronger. Optimally, you would like to become stronger. The pain of addressing your trauma will be yet another challenge to overcome. No need to run from it. No need to sugarcoat or disguise it. It is what it is, but it won't control you.*

*It's not the adversity that defines you, either. The defining moment is in how you respond to that adversity. Rather than avoiding it, embrace the struggle and feel the pain because pain is just the first step of the process. As you suffer through the pain, you'll discover your passion. Your passion will force you to fight not only against what had caused you pain but also for what your ultimate purpose is in life. Once you discover your purpose and begin to live in it, it will force you to regain your power. And after you regain your power over yourself and over the outside world, you'll soon be on your way to finding your peace.*

*Pain to passion. Passion to purpose. Purpose to power. Power to peace. That is the process of perseverance.*

## What We Can Learn from Reggie's Journey:

Reggie's story reframes what perseverance truly means. His life demonstrates that resilience isn't about suppressing pain—it's about learning to work with it, to turn awareness into growth, and growth into impact. Through his journey, we see how trauma can coexist with excellence, how cultural context shapes healing, and how vulnerability can become a source of authentic leadership.

**The Power of Psychological Safety in Leadership:** Reggie reminds us that healing requires environments where people feel safe to take risks, admit mistakes, and show vulnerability. In business and leadership, creating psychological safety doesn't only support trauma survivors—it drives innovation, collaboration, and long-term performance.

**Recognizing Self-sabotage in Professional Settings:** Trauma can manifest as perfectionism, mistrust, or reluctance to delegate. Reggie's awareness of these patterns shows that identifying and addressing them is essential for breaking cycles that limit professional growth.

**Internal Validation over External Metrics:** Promotions, titles, and recognition can motivate, but they cannot substitute for authentic self-worth. Reggie's journey demonstrates that sustainable performance comes when leaders ground themselves in purpose rather than in external validation.

**Healing as Ongoing Professional Development:** Just as leaders commit to lifelong learning in their fields, trauma recovery requires continuous attention. Reggie's practices—therapy, mindfulness, and intentional reflection—are reminders that emotional wellness is inseparable from professional success.

**Entrepreneurship and Agency:** For Reggie, entrepreneurship was not only about profit; it was about reclaiming independence, voice, and identity. His experience underscores that pursuing ventures aligned with personal healing can strengthen confidence, clarity, and influence in business.

## Reflections for the Reader

- *In what ways might your past experiences be shaping how you lead, manage conflict, or relate to authority today?*

- *Do you notice patterns—overworking, distrust, perfectionism—that once helped you cope but now limit your growth?*

- *Where are you depending on external markers of success (titles, recognition, income) instead of cultivating confidence from within?*

- ***Who in your circle offers genuine psychological safety, someone you can talk with openly and without judgment?***

____________________

____________________

____________________

____________________

- ***What steady practices—journaling, mindfulness, coaching, or wellness routines—could strengthen both your healing and your professional presence?***

____________________

____________________

____________________

____________________

Reggie Ford's inspiring story reminds us that leadership is not defined solely by achievement but by the courage to confront and transform the wounds that shape us. His life and work illustrate that healing trauma is not a personal luxury; it is a professional imperative. By integrating intentionality and compassion into our daily lives, we can expand both our capacity for healing and our capacity for impact in the workplace.

CHAPTER 16

# The Healing Power of Storytelling

*She could barely get the words out the first time she told her story. She hesitated, her breath catching in her throat as shame and fear rose up like a tide. Would they judge her? Would they turn away? For years, she had convinced herself that silence was safer, that if she buried her pain deep enough, it might disappear.*

What you've just read may feel familiar. Many survivors describe this exact moment—the terrifying pause between silence and speech—as the hardest step in their healing journey. It takes extraordinary courage to say the first words out loud. Yet once spoken, those words often open the door to something powerful: connection, empathy, and even freedom.

That is the power of storytelling. Psychologists Richard Tedeschi and Lawrence Calhoun have even given this process a name: posttraumatic growth. Their research shows that many survivors not only recover but also go on to experience greater strength, deeper relationships, and renewed purpose.

As you've read the stories of professionals who've overcome trauma, it's clear that healing is not a solitary journey. Each of these individuals found strength not only within themselves but also through the power of shared experience. Their stories remind us that, whereas trauma may have shaped parts of our lives, it doesn't have to define our future. Trauma is something that happened to us; it is not who we are.

Leadership research reinforces this point. Many successful entrepreneurs have shown that early adversity, when voiced, can become the foundation of extraordinary influence. Their authority was strengthened, not diminished, by the courage to tell their stories.

By sharing our experiences, we reclaim our narrative. We begin to separate our identity from the pain of the past, opening ourselves to growth and transformation.

## How Sharing Heals Us All

Stories have the power to transform. When we share our experiences, fears, triumphs, and setbacks, we not only give voice to our pain but also invite others into our healing process.

Neuroscientists confirm what survivors often describe: Trauma changes how the brain encodes memory and processes stress. Other studies suggest it can even leave chemical "marks" on our genes, altering how our bodies respond to stress for decades and sometimes across generations. Yet when people tell their stories in safe, supportive spaces, the act itself can help regulate stress responses, interrupt cycles of silence, and protect the next generation.

Think about the stories in this book. Each one is a testament to inner strength, showing that the path forward from trauma can be one of growth and triumph. However, beyond personal healing, a deeper theme is at play: communal healing.

When we share our stories, we break the silence that trauma often demands. We show that pain is not something to be hidden but something that can be overcome. We allow others to see that they, too, can rise from their struggles and find a better, happier version of themselves on the other side.

Healing happens in connection. When one person speaks, another listens. And when we listen to someone else's story, we begin to recognize pieces of our own.

In every interview I conducted for this book, there was a moment of deep connectional shift in energy when someone realized that they weren't alone. Despite different circumstances, we are all connected by our humanity. We are not alone in our suffering nor in our healing.

There is something incredibly empowering about hearing another person's story and realizing, *I've felt that too.*

## Building a Supportive Community

Healing rarely happens in isolation. Although personal reflection is essential, one of the most profound ways to begin the healing process is by connecting with others.

Trauma often isolates us, convincing us that our struggles are unique or too heavy to share. But when we step into spaces of connection—whether through sharing our story with a trusted friend, joining a support group, or simply being honest about what we're going through, we begin to break down those walls.

Community is not only about being heard; it's about hearing others, too. There's immense power in realizing that you're not alone and that others have walked similar paths and found ways to heal and grow.

The workplace offers one example. A *Harvard Business Review* article described what happens when organizations ignore trauma: It creates what psychologists call "institutional betrayal," a secondary wound caused by silence or inaction. But when leaders acknowledge the pain in their teams and respond with empathy and consistency, they build trust and psychological safety. The same principle holds true in our personal lives.

When we acknowledge each other's struggles and offer support, we create the conditions where healing can happen.

If you're unsure where to begin, start small. Seek out safe spaces where vulnerability is met with empathy and understanding. This could be a close-knit group of friends, a mentor who has been through similar challenges, or an online community where shared experiences create a sense of support.

Building a supportive community isn't about quantity; it's about quality. A single meaningful relationship, where you feel seen and heard, can be more healing than a room full of acquaintances.

For many of the individuals you've met in these pages, finding support was the turning point in their journey. Whether it was family, close friends, colleagues, or professional networks, they found strength in knowing they weren't alone.

If you are at the beginning of your healing journey, take a moment to think about the people in your life who support you. If those relationships don't feel supportive, consider seeking out a community, whether in person or online, where you can share your story and hear the stories of others.

Healing begins in connection.

## Vulnerability and Empathy

Vulnerability is powerful. Each story in this book has a thread of vulnerability running through it. The courage to open up about trauma, to speak about the parts of life that are often left unspoken, is what makes these stories so impactful.

Empathy, in turn, is what allows us to connect with those stories. When we hear someone's vulnerability, it stirs something within us. It allows us to see parts of ourselves in their experiences. Empathy is the bridge that connects us—it transforms personal stories into collective healing experiences.

Each person you've read about in this book has, at some point, allowed themselves to be vulnerable. In doing so, they've invited others into their story. They've shown that it's OK to acknowledge the hard things —the things we wish weren't part of our past —and to move forward with compassion for ourselves.

Empathy goes both ways. By embracing our own vulnerability and sharing our stories, we allow others to empathize with us. We create a space for others to feel safe in their own vulnerability. Each shared story sparks the courage for another to be told.

## Strength in Numbers

A common theme in all the stories shared in this book is endurance. Each person you've read about has shown remarkable inner strength in the face of adversity. That strength wasn't developed in isolation. It was shaped by the people around them: the communities that offered support, the friends who believed in them, and the mentors who guided them.

Endurance is not something you're simply born with; it's something you build over time, much like training a muscle. As physical strength comes from repeated effort and rest, emotional strength grows from facing challenges, learning from them, and learning from others when needed. Entrepreneurs understand this well. Recent business research describes adaptability as a "toolbox" of practical strategies, ranging from reframing challenges to drawing on support systems. Storytelling is one of the most powerful tools in that kit. By putting words to adversity, we transform it from something that isolates us into something that connects us.

Collective strength, the idea that we are stronger together than we are alone, is key to overcoming trauma. When we share our stories and support one another, we create communities where growth and recovery can flourish.

You don't have to go through your healing journey alone. Reach out. Find others who share similar experiences. Create a space where stories can be told, where vulnerability is met with empathy, and where growth is honored. That's where true healing begins.

## Your Own Story Is Still Being Written

Now that you've heard the stories of others, I encourage you to reflect on your own.

Your story is still being written. You hold the pen.

Whether you've faced childhood trauma or not, we all have experiences that shape who we are and how we move through the world.

The stories in this book are meant to inspire you to take ownership of your own narrative.

*What part of your story is ready for change?*

*What fears, beliefs, or habits have you carried from childhood into your professional and personal life?*

*What patterns have been repeating in your relationships, your work, and your self-perception?*

Your past does not define you. Your choices do.

This book isn't about telling you what steps to take. It's about showing you that healing is possible—and that your story, whatever it may be, has the potential to inspire others.

You are part of this collective journey toward resilience. Your experiences matter. Your healing matters.

As you move forward, I leave you with this: The past may have written the first chapters of your life. But the ending? That's yours to create.

CHAPTER 17

# On Writing Your Next Chapter

The end of a book is never truly the end of a story. It's a pause, a breath, before the next sentence is written. Now, as you turn these final pages, I want you to remember something important: Your story is still unfolding.

The stories you've read are not only about trauma; they are about transformation. They are about resilience, courage, and the undeniable strength that exists within each of us when we decide that our past does not get the final say in who we become.

This book has taken you through the journeys of other people who have faced deep wounds, struggled in silence, and fought their way toward healing. But the most important journey is the one you take from here. What will you do with what you've learned? How will you take the insights, reflections, and moments of recognition you've experienced and apply them to your own life?

One of the most powerful truths to embrace is that you are not defined by what happened to you; you are defined by what you choose to do next. Many of the people you've met in these pages once believed their past would always control their future. They thought their trauma had written the ending before they even had the chance to pick up the pen. But through self-awareness, support, and the courage to face what they once feared, they rewrote their stories.

You have the same power. Your trauma, hardships, and past experiences may have shaped you, but they do not own you. You can step out of the patterns that have kept you stuck. You can rewrite the narratives that have told you you're not enough. You can choose healing, growth, and a new way forward.

It won't be easy. Change rarely is. But every step you take toward healing is a step toward reclaiming yourself.

As you close this book, take a moment to reflect. What patterns have you noticed in your life that you're ready to change? What beliefs about yourself no longer serve you? What would it feel like to let go of the weight you've been carrying? These questions are invitations, not obligations. You don't have to have all the answers right now. You don't have to fix everything at once. Healing is not a single decision—it's a series of choices made over and over again. And the first choice is this: believing that you deserve a new chapter.

You have the power to shape what comes next. You have the power to take what has happened and transform it into wisdom, strength, and purpose. You have the power to stand in the truth of your experience without shame, fear, or apology.

Your past is a chapter, not the whole book. Now, you get to decide how the next pages will unfold.

When you're ready, pick up the pen.

EPILOGUE

# Gone Too Soon—a Story Unfinished

I want to close this book by telling you about a dear childhood friend of mine, whom I will call John (a pseudonym). He was one of the kindest and most giving people I have ever known. His kindness to others belied what he had been through in his youth. Unbeknownst to me, he had his own story of childhood trauma, childhood abuse, and bullying that shaped his entire life. It affected his career choice and his drive for accomplishment and motivated his determination to be kind to everyone. He carried his story in silence for decades while at the same time becoming incredibly successful. But a few years ago, he made a decision: He was going to write down his story.

He poured himself into a manuscript. Page after page, he began to tell the truth he had never shared before. It was long, raw, and courageous. For the first time, he was ready to make his pain visible. He told me he planned to publish it. He wanted to give his story to the world.

Then, before he could, he was gone. He died suddenly of cardiac arrest, gone way too soon—his untold story literally taken to his grave.

I was left still holding his manuscript to review.

I have thought about him often since. I think about what it must have taken for him to finally put words to a lifetime of silence. I think about what it cost him to carry that pain alone for so long. And I think about how unresolved trauma can weigh on the body in ways we may never fully understand. Was he to be another statistic on the ACE Health Outcomes chart? One of those people who was 275 percent more likely to die of a heart attack due to their past trauma.

Perhaps that is why I feel compelled to honor him here. His words, although unfinished, stand as a testament to courage. They remind us that silence takes its toll and that waiting to share our truth can sometimes mean never getting the chance.

If you are holding back your own story, let his serve as an invitation: Don't wait.

Don't assume there will be a better time, or a safer season, or the "right" words.

Begin now.

John's story may never be fully finished on paper. But in another sense, it doesn't have to be. Every time one of us chooses honesty over silence, or healing over hiding, his legacy continues. His courage to begin can become our courage to continue.

So, dear reader, I leave you with his reminder: Your story matters, and the world needs to hear it.

Don't let it go untold.

MENTAL HEALTH AND TRAUMA RECOVERY RESOURCES

# Crisis and Mental Health Helplines

Healing from trauma is not a solo journey. Support is essential, whether it comes from mental health professionals, crisis intervention teams, or self-guided tools. The following resources provide immediate support, long-term therapy options, and educational materials to help individuals navigate trauma's impact.

These resources offer immediate support for those experiencing distress or crisis situations.

# Crisis and Mental Health Helplines listing

| Resource | Contact Information | Description |
|---|---|---|
| 988 Suicide & Crisis Lifeline | Call or text 988 | Provides free, 24/7 support for individuals in distress or suicidal crisis. Chat is available at 988lifeline.org |
| SAMHSA's National Helpline | 1-800-662-HELP (4357) | Confidential, free help for substance abuse and mental health treatment referrals. Text your zip code to 435748 (HELP4U) for local services. |
| Disaster Distress Helpline | 1-800-985-5990 | Provides crisis counseling for those experiencing distress related to natural or human-caused disasters. |
| Veterans Crisis Line | Dial 988, then press 1 | Specialized crisis support for veterans. Text 838255 for text support. |
| FindTreatment .gov | Online at www. findtreatment. gov | A tool for locating mental health and substance abuse treatment providers nationwide. |
| Early Serious Mental Illness Treatment Locator | Online at samhsa.gov/ esmi-treatment-locator | Helps individuals find early intervention and specialized treatment for severe mental health disorders. |

# Healing Housing

Writing *Dealing with Healing* was one way I could honor all the women who have come through the doors of Healing Housing to write their new story of hope. Healing Housing is a 501(c)(3) nonprofit based in Nashville, Tennessee, providing recovery housing and comprehensive services for women without financial resources who are healing from alcohol and drug addiction. Most of the women served have experienced trauma, poverty, or incarceration and are at risk of homelessness when they arrive from treatment centers or jail.

Since opening its doors in 2017, Healing Housing has evolved from a recovery residence into a comprehensive program that offers safe housing, therapy, financial guidance, life skills training, and spiritual support. Their mission is simple but profound: to provide the tools, structure, and unconditional love women need to maintain sobriety, find stability, and rebuild their lives.

To learn more, donate, or get involved, visit healinghousing.org.

# Understanding Trauma and Its Impact

Healing begins with awareness, and sometimes the first step is simply learning more about what trauma does to the body, mind, and spirit. The following resources offer research-based insight into how trauma shapes mental and physical health as well as tools and guidance for treatment and recovery.

- **CDC–Kaiser Adverse Childhood Experiences (ACE) Study** (https://www.cdc.gov/violenceprevention/aces/about.html)

  A foundational study on how early trauma influences long-term health and career outcomes.

- **National Child Traumatic Stress Network (NCTSN)** (https://www.nctsn.org/)

  This organization offers educational materials and research on childhood trauma, treatment approaches, and best practices.

- **National Institutes of Health PTSD Research** (https://pmc.ncbi.nlm.nih.gov/articles/PMC5632781/)

  A comprehensive study examining PTSD and mental health impacts globally.

# Workplace Trauma and Leadership Support

Trauma doesn't stay at home; it shows up in the workplace, too. From stress and burnout to leadership blind spots and toxic cultures, unaddressed trauma can erode professional environments. These resources provide research, guidance, and practical strategies for building workplaces where both leaders and employees can thrive:

- **American Psychological Association: Striving for Mental Health Excellence Workplace Guide** (https://www.apa.org/topics/healthy-workplaces/mental-health/striving-mental-health-excellence-workplace-guide.pdf)

  A free tool for leaders to help their team reduce professional stress, burnout, and workplace trauma.

- **Workplace Bullying Institute** (https://workplacebullying.org/)

  A resource for employees facing workplace bullying, offering support and strategies for intervention.

- **The National Alliance on Mental Illness (NAMI)** (https://www.nami.org/)

  Provides information on mental health in the workplace, including employer policies and employee rights.

# Understanding Your DISC Profile and Behavioral Tendencies

DISC personality assessments provide insight into behavioral tendencies, leadership styles, and workplace dynamics, helping individuals navigate relationships effectively.

# The Four DISC Styles

Dominant (D)
Influencing (I)
Steady (S)
Conscientious (C)

**Dominant (D): The Driver**

If you're a D, you're probably decisive, results-oriented, and not afraid to take charge. You like clarity, you move fast, and you'd rather fix a problem than talk about it for hours.

**What it looks like in action:** You get things done. You speak your mind. You're not here for fluff.

**What to watch for:** Ds can sometimes bulldoze people without meaning to. Slowing down and listening fully is a skill worth building.

**Influencing (I): The Connector**

If you're an I, you're probably expressive, optimistic, and energized by people. You bring big energy into the room and often find yourself leading without even trying.

**What it looks like in action:** You motivate others, you love to collaborate, and you're great at building relationships.

**What to watch for:** It can sometimes skim the surface or chase new ideas without follow-through. Learning to stay grounded and focused can help deepen both work and connection.

**Steady (S): The Stabilizer**

If you're an S, you're probably calm, dependable, and motivated by harmony. You value consistency, loyalty, and making sure everyone feels supported. You don't rush decisions—you prefer steady progress and clear expectations.

**What it looks like in action:** You're a great listener. You show up consistently. You keep teams grounded and functioning smoothly, especially during change or stress.

**What to watch for:** Ss can sometimes avoid conflict or resist change, even when it's necessary. Practicing speaking up sooner and embracing discomfort can help you grow without losing your steadiness.

**Conscientious (C): The Analyst**

If you're a C, you're probably thoughtful, detail-oriented, and driven by accuracy. You value logic, quality, and doing things the right way. You like clear systems and time to think things through.

**What it looks like in action:** You plan carefully, ask smart questions, and deliver high-quality work. You spot errors others miss and bring structure to complexity.

**What to watch for:** Cs can sometimes over-analyze or hold back waiting for perfection. Learning to take action with "good enough" information can increase impact without sacrificing excellence.

**Scan the QR code below to learn more about Write a New Story and how to work with Oliva Smith.**

# Building a Trauma-Informed Support System

Healing is a continuous process that benefits from community support. Whether you're seeking a therapist, peer support, or self-help resources, the following tools can help you build a stronger foundation for recovery.

- **Therapy Finder**: **Psychology Today** (www.psychologytoday.com/us/therapists) Search for licensed therapists based on specialty, insurance, and location.
- **Alcoholics Anonymous (AA) & Narcotics Anonymous (NA) (www.na.org/)**— Support groups for individuals recovering from substance use disorders.
- **National Domestic Violence Hotline**—Call **1-800-799-7233** or text **START** to **88788** for confidential support related to domestic violence.

Understanding trauma is only the beginning. Healing takes shape when you act on that awareness, whether by seeking professional support, practicing self-reflection, or leaning on a community that understands. Each of these choices helps you reclaim your story and move forward with greater clarity.

Healing doesn't require erasing the past; it's about creating a future where your experiences contribute to wisdom and strength rather than limitation. If one of these resources feels relevant to you, take the next step.

# Bibliography

Alcoholics Anonymous. (n.d.). *Alcoholics Anonymous.* Retrieved October 13, 2025, from https://www.aa.org

Alhassen, S. (2021). Intergenerational trauma transmission in mice. *Communications Biology, 4*(1), 783. https://pubmed.ncbi.nlm.nih.gov/34168265/

American Psychological Association. (n.d.). *Healthy workplaces and workplace stress guide.* Retrieved October 13, 2025, from https://www.apa.org/topics/healthy-workplaces

Centers for Disease Control and Prevention (CDC). (2012, February 1). *Child abuse and neglect are serious public health problems.* https://archive.cdc.gov/#/details?url=https://www.cdc.gov/media/releases/2012/p0201_child_abuse.html

Centers for Disease Control and Prevention (CDC). (n.d.). *Adverse Childhood Experiences (ACE) study.* Retrieved October 13, 2025, from https://www.cdc.gov/aces/about/index.html

Disaster Distress Helpline. (n.d.). Retrieved October 13, 2025, from https://disasterdistress.samhsa.gov

Felitti, V. J., Anda, R. F., Nordenberg, D., Williamson, D. F., Spitz, A. M., Edwards, V., Koss, M. P., & Marks, J. S. (1998, May). Relationship of childhood abuse and household dysfunction to many of the leading causes of death in adults. The Adverse Childhood Experiences (ACE)

study. *American Journal of Preventive Medicine, 14*(4), 245–58. https://www.doi.org/10.1016/s0749-3797(98)00017-8.

FindTreatment.gov. (n.d.). Retrieved October 13, 2025, from https://findtreatment.gov/

Gloria, C. T., Steinhardt, M. A., & Yi, M. (2022). Resilience in leadership: Learning from trauma-transformed leaders. *Creative Education, 13*(5), 1667–1682. https://pubmed.ncbi.nlm.nih.gov/24962138/

Hughes, K., Bellis, M. A., Hardcastle, K. A., Sethi, D., Butchart, A., Mikton, C., Jones, L., & Dunne, M. P. (2017). The effect of multiple adverse childhood experiences on health: A systematic review and meta-analysis. *The Lancet Public Health, 2*(8), e356–e366. https://doi.org/10.1016/S2468-2667(17)30118-4

Laricchiuta, D. (2023, May). The neurobiological profile of trauma: Brain–body integration. *Neuroscience & Biobehavioral Reviews, 145.* https://www.sciencedirect.com/science/article/pii/S0149763423000027

Manning, K. (2022, March 31). We need trauma-informed workplaces. *Harvard Business Review.* https://hbr.org/2022/03/we-need-trauma-informed-workplaces

Mandated Reporter. (2022). *The state of child abuse in 2022.* https://mandatedreporter.com/blog/the-state-of-child-abuse-in-2022

National Alliance on Mental Illness (NAMI). (n.d.). *Mental health and employment resources.* Retrieved October 13, 2025, from https://www.nami.org/Your-Journey/Individuals-with-Mental-Illness/Employment

National Child Traumatic Stress Network. (n.d.). *Resources on childhood trauma.* Retrieved October 13, 2025, from https://www.nctsn.org

National Domestic Violence Hotline. (n.d.). *Get help.* Retrieved October 13, 2025, from https://www.thehotline.org

National Institute of Mental Health. (n.d.). *Post-traumatic stress disorder (PTSD)*. Retrieved October 13, 2025, from https://www.nimh.nih.gov/health/topics/post-traumatic-stress-disorder-ptsd

Narcotics Anonymous. (n.d.). *Narcotics Anonymous.* Retrieved October 13, 2025, from https://na.org/

Nie, Y. (2022, November 14). Emerging trends in epigenetic and childhood trauma studies. *Frontiers in Psychiatry.* https://www.frontiersin.org/articles/10.3389/fpsyt.2022.925273/full

Psychology Today. (n.d.). *Therapist finder.* Retrieved October 13, 2025, from https://www.psychologytoday.com/us/therapists

SAMHSA. (n.d.). *Early serious mental illness (ESMI) treatment locator.* Retrieved October 13, 2025, from https://www.samhsa.gov/esmi-treatment-locator

SAMHSA. (n.d.). *National helpline.* Retrieved October 13, 2025, from https://www.samhsa.gov/find-help/national-helpline

SAMHSA. (n.d.). *Trauma & violence resource center.* Retrieved October 13, 2025, from https://www.samhsa.gov/trauma-violence

*Scientific American.* (2022, July 1). How parents' trauma leaves biological traces in children. https://www.scientificamerican.com/article/how-parents-rsquo-trauma-leaves-biological-traces-in-children

Simarasl, N. (2024). Resilience-building coping strategies and actionable tools for entrepreneurs. *Journal of Business Research, 68*(5). https://www.sciencedirect.com/science/article/pii/S0007681324000880

Suicide & Crisis Lifeline. (n.d.). *988 Suicide & Crisis Lifeline.* Retrieved October 13, 2025, from https://988lifeline.org/

Tat Life. (n.d.). *The Adverse Childhood Experiences study: The largest, most important public health study you never heard of began in an obesity clinic.*

Retrieved October 13, 2025, from https://tatlife.com/the-adverse-childhood-experiences-study-the-largest-most-important-public-health-study-you-never-heard-of-began-in-an-obesity-clinic/

Tedeschi, R. G., & Calhoun, L. G. (1996). The Posttraumatic Growth Inventory: Measuring the positive legacy of trauma. *Journal of Traumatic Stress, 9*(3), 455–471. https://pubmed.ncbi.nlm.nih.gov/8827649/

Tedeschi, R. G., & Calhoun, L. G. (2004). TARGET ARTICLE: Posttraumatic Growth: Conceptual foundations and empirical evidence. *Psychological Inquiry, 15*(1), 1–18. https://doi.org/10.1207/s15327965pli1501_01

U.S. Department of Veterans Affairs. (n.d.). *Veterans crisis line.* Retrieved October 13, 2025, from https://www.veteranscrisisline.net

Workplace Bullying Institute. (n.d.). *Research and resources.* Retrieved October 13, 2025, from https://workplacebullying.org

Yu, X., Yang, W., Han, F., & Cui, T. (2022). The nonlinear relationship between adversity and entrepreneurial success: Evidence from China. *Journal of Business Research, 146,* 105–116. https://doi.org/10.1016/j.jbusres.2022.03.019

www.ingramcontent.com/pod-product-compliance
Ingram Content Group UK Ltd.
Pitfield, Milton Keynes, MK11 3LW, UK
UKHW062302290726
14090UKWH00017B/842

9 798993 929217